Return to Java Ross
thank you

DEVELOPING YOUR PEOPLE

GW00632302

Suzy Siddons specialises in the psychology of communication. After working for a West London Psychological Service and spending several years as a full-time writer, she entered the information technology industry as a training officer – this was the easiest way to get a free word processor! One and a half years later she was headhunted by a large computer manufacturer to join its sales training department, initially to set up and run training for their network of dealers and distributors, and later to deliver and originate courses for the sales, marketing, support services and field services divisions of the company. These courses covered a wide range of behaviour and business skills. Since founding her own training company in 1987 she has worked with a wide range of clients, consulting and training in the behavioural skills needed in business. Her other titles for the CIPD are *Delivering Training* (1997), *Presentation Skills* (1999) and *Encouraging Positive Participation* (1999), a trainers' kitbag.

The Chartered Institute of Personnel and Development is the leading publisher of books and reports for personnel and training professionals, students, and for all those concerned with the effective management and development of people at work. For details of all our titles, please contact the Publishing Department:

tel. 020-8263 3387

fax 020-8263 3850

e-mail publish@cipd.co.uk

The catalogue of all CIPD titles can be viewed on the CIPD website:

www.cipd.co.uk/publications

DEVELOPING YOUR PEOPLE

PAIN-FREE SOLUTIONS FOR BUSY MANAGERS

Suzy Siddons

Chartered Institute of Personnel and Development

© Suzy Siddons, 2001

First published 2001

All rights reserved. No part of this publication may be reproduced, stored in
an information storage and retrieval system, or transmitted in any form or
by any means, electronic, mechanical, photocopying, recording or otherwise, without written permission of the Chartered Institute of Personnel and
Development, CIPD House, Camp Road, London SW19 4UX.

Phototypeset by The Comp-Room, Aylesbury and printed in the UK by
the Cromwell Press, Trowbridge

British Library Cataloguing in Publication Data
A catalogue record for this book is available from the British Library

ISBN 0-85292-889-0

The views expressed in this book are the author's own, and may not
necessarily reflect those of the CIPD.

Chartered Institute of Personnel and Development
CIPD House, Camp Road, London SW19 4UX
Tel: 020-8971 9000 Fax: 020-8263 3333
E-mail: cipd@cipd.co.uk
Website: www.cipd.co.uk
Incorporated by Royal Charter. Registered charity no. 1079797.

CONTENTS

ACKNOWLEDGEMENTS

My most heartfelt thanks go to a great many people for the help and advice they have given me – not least the managers I have met over the years who have shared their ideas, triumphs and worries with me.

Particular thanks go to Peter Vacher, not only for his encouragement, but also for allowing me to quote from his excellent 'ideas document', which he sent to me to unblock my thought processes.

My thanks, as always, to my husband David, who, with Bonzo our cat, has supported me throughout.

And finally to Anne Cordwent – the best editor in the world. Without her none of this would have been possible.

INTRODUCTION

In a perfect world, this would be your day as a manager:

You arrive at work to find the day ahead is beautifully planned out. The right proportion of your time is allocated for analysis, planning and strategic matters. While you are doing this, your team is competently performing all their tasks and duties. The right proportion of your time is to be spent on talking to your staff about the progress of their tasks and jobs, encouraging, organising and correcting as you go. The right proportion of your time will be spent on developing your staff in all manner of ways. *There are no glitches or hitches, there is an unlimited training budget, no customer interrupts the even tenor of your day with unreasonable demands, there is unlimited support for everything you propose. You have no tasks that are not management tasks, and, what is more, you have a dedicated team of secretaries, gofers, administrators, trainers, psychiatrists and logistics experts who will jump at your every command. As well as unfettered access to meeting rooms and quiet spaces.*

Oh, wouldn't it be luvverly!

What is more likely to happen is this:

You arrive at work to find that members of your staff are ill or unavoidably absent. The last project you were involved with is running late. The meeting you hoped to hold at 10.00am has been moved to tomorrow (the meeting room wasn't available anyway). Two other members of your staff have immediate and pressing problems that you need to sort out. You are three weeks late on finishing all the staff assessment interviews and you have discovered that the new 'expert' who has just joined your team hasn't a clue how the software you are using is working and can't find the fax machine. You have a severely curtailed training budget and you are personally targeted to make all those numbers by the end of Q2. You have limited help. There is no time to think – let alone a quiet place in which to do so.

As for developing your team – well, dream on ... how often do firemen develop their teams while fighting a blaze?

Every manager knows that his or her strength lies in the strengths of the team.

Here's a quote from the ex-CEO of a huge publishing and printing company:

> *We had a computer company in Boston, USA. Its development needs were running away with the funds from our UK company, especially as, in 1983, we were getting only $1.04 for each £1 we sent across. We wrote a business plan which was to be our prospectus for selling the company. There were 10 chapters. They covered such topics as markets, the competition, the financials, sales projections, the risks, the uniqueness of the product, the intellectual property and so on. But when I took the document to companies which included Kodak, 3M, Dupont, Fujifilm and leading US newspapers, the first thing that every CEO turned to was the chapter on the company's people. If they could not see that we employed the right people, then they weren't interested in reading further.*

Few of us can just go out and recruit who we want, when we want. So where do we find the right people? How can we find the right mix of skills in our team that will free us up for all the other million and one tasks we must perform from day to day?

The answer is obvious – train, cultivate and develop them yourself. *But*, the real secret is finding clever ways to develop our teams that are not overelaborate, costly or time-consuming!

As a busy manager you are likely to spend much of your day endlessly sorting out problems, encouraging people and talking through their worries. Do you sometimes get to the end of the day and wonder what you have achieved? Do you ever stop to consider that you have probably been training by stealth all along?

The first really excellent manager I worked for was extraordinary at doing this. This was in the golden days when new technology was ramping up – his team was growing like Topsy (doubling every six months in fact). We were all keen as mustard, but sadly lacking in experience – and when it comes to keeping up with rapid change, enthusiasm is not enough; we needed the wisdom, skills and insight that only experience can bring. What did he do? Well in one week alone he had sent two of us off to 'sit by Nellie' (similar to being an apprentice) where we learned first-hand just what our jobs entailed. He sent another team member to a seminar, he personally coached me on how to run meetings and he brought an expert in to train our administrator on the accounting system that had just been introduced into the company – an enormous amount of development, and, apart from the coaching, not requiring huge amounts of time on his part.

The writer Chamfort in *Charactêres et Anecdotes* (1771) wisely remarked that 'Man arrives as a novice at each stage of his life.'

How did you get to be a manager? Well, when you joined your first company or took your first job, you were probably chosen for your technical, physical or specialist skills. Sadly, at the time, your personal, company or business skills may not have been as sharp, since you were in a situation where the mysterious workings of this new environment were not well known to you.

As time passed you probably found that the razor edge of these technical, physical or specialist skills became considerably blunter. Technology changed, your job changed, new products and markets arrived and you and the business world moved on. Looking on the bright side, over the same period of time your company, business and personal skills undoubtedly increased as you got to know the company and market you were working with and the multitude of people connected with this. With this growth in business and personal skills came experience, confidence and a huge network of colleagues, customers and suppliers.

Technical v business skills (1)

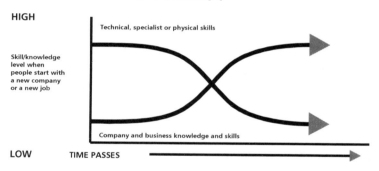

HIGH

Technical, specialist or physical skills

Skill/knowledge level when people start with a new company or a new job

Company and business knowledge and skills

LOW   TIME PASSES

It is just this skill increase that led to you becoming a manager. So how did you gain these skills? How did you develop the ability to lead a group and understand and handle the complexities of your business career? Most probably you had the ambition and drive to take advantage of the experiences and changes that surround all business people. Most probably you found people who acted as mentors and showed you the ropes. You may have taken training courses to sharpen particular skills; whatever your route, you certainly played a large part in dealing yourself your present manager's job. In other words – you developed yourself.

The eternal problem

This brings us to the eternal problem that faces all managers: 'How do I keep the specialist, physical or technological skills of my group high, and how do I ramp up their company, business and personal skills as quickly and effectively as possible?'

Technical v business skills (2)

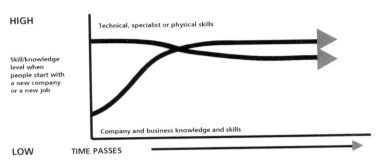

This is usually followed by the heartfelt plea: 'How on earth can I do this? I'm not a trainer and I'm not paid to be a trainer, and what's more I've got so much else to do!'

The role of development skills in the manager's toolbox

The major skills that every manager uses are:

■ **planning** – working out what needs to be done in macro, looking at timescales and resources, weaving together the multiplicity of business tasks that face you and your team; strategising for the future and assessing risks

■ **organising** – defining how, when, where and by whom it should be done, giving the right jobs to the right people, sorting out the day-to-day running of your team and delegating where necessary

■ **motivating** – persuading your team to fulfil their tasks and keeping them energetic, healthy and on the ball, working out a successful rewards system, praising and giving confidence

- **controlling** – making sure that time/quality/budget commitments are met, keeping the team together, ensuring that people are treated fairly
- **developing** – helping the people you manage to grow in experience, gain necessary skills and climb the ladder of success, looking at people's skill sets and the needs of the business, encouraging personal and business growth.

It is true that all of these skills will always be needed; but, in today's lean, mean organisations the need for managers to develop the individuals within their teams has become an imperative. A manager is only as good as his or her team, and when the team stays in the same place, growth is not possible.

Job specifications are becoming broader. Single-skill and specialist jobs are becoming rarer. As the use of technology increases, there is a constant need for knowledge and skill updating – and all of this on top of increasing workloads and the day-to-day complexity of business tasks, not to mention the rapid changes in markets, legislation and business practices.

The cure

Developing Your People: Pain-free solutions for busy managers takes you through the choices available to you for developing your people, no matter what type of business you work in, from public to private sector; these are options lying on your doorstep. There is an emphasis on cost-effectiveness and practicality. Above all it does not require you as a manager to act as a trainer, instead it looks at the resources that are currently available, suggests simple ways of capitalising on the skills already existing in your team, company, business environment and the outside world. It also gives practical hints and tips on how to make these recipes and methodologies really work.

So is there a process that managers can use to develop their people effectively? There certainly is:

Development process

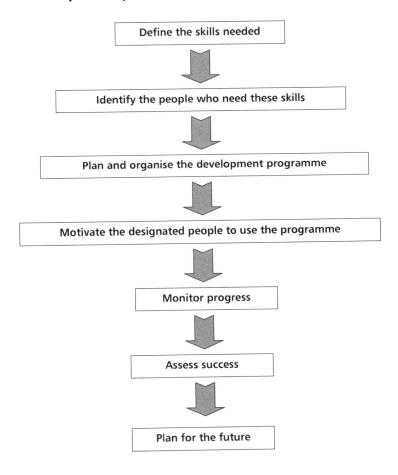

Developing Your People follows this process through.

Section 1 will help you to:

■ define the skills needed and who might need them
■ find situations where development needs may arise
■ look at the groups of skills that may be needed
■ decide who might be affected.

Section 2 helps you with the general planning and organisation of a development programme and how to motivate the people who will be affected by it:

- how to design a programme
- how to measure success
- how to look at attitudes to learning and development
- how you can motivate the reluctant 'developee'.

Section 3 looks at the options, methods and resources you will need. Each subsection contains the following:

- what the option is – a definition
- a table showing the pros and cons and where this particular option is most useful
- where you can find help
- how to set it up
- how to check whether learning has happened
- more activities (cross-referenced)
- hints and tips.

Section 4 looks at ways you could develop yourself and, more importantly, what you should be concentrating on when your team is fired up.

FIRST STEPS

> 'Each new season grows from the leftovers from the past. That is the essence of change, and change is the basic law.'
> Hal Borland, *Sundial of the Seasons* (1964)

Just as we all grow and develop through our lives from infancy through childhood and adolescence to adulthood, so changes in our business lives will force growth and development. These changes can broadly be listed under four main headings:

- **external change** – factors and events that are on the outside of your company that have an impact on the way your whole company works and trades
- **internal change** – factors and events happening within your company that have an impact on the way your whole company works and trades
- **group change** – factors and events happening within your company that have an impact on the way your management group works
- **personal change** – factors and events happening within your group that have an impact on the way the individuals in your group work.

When starting a development plan for your team it is a useful exercise to look at the 'drivers of change' that affect your company. A list like the one in the following table would start the thinking process off:

Drivers of change

External change	Internal change	Group change	Personal change
✓ **Technological**	✓ **Reorganisation**	✓ **Redundancy**	✓ **Promotion**
❑ New plant and	❑ Takeovers		
machinery	❑ Collaboration	✓ **Cost-cutting**	✓ **Job change**
❑ New IT	❑ Partnerships		
❑ New methods	❑ Upsizing	✓ **Groups amal-**	✓ **New tasks**
❑ New infrastruc-	❑ Downsizing	**gamate**	
ture	❑ New working		✓ **Need to**
	practices	✓ **New projects**	**delegate**
✓ **Environment**	❑ New premises		
❑ Health and	❑ ISO standards	✓ **New group**	✓ **New boss**
safety laws		**members**	
❑ Hazards	✓ **Introduction of**		✓ **Change from**
	new products	✓ **New products**	**'backroom**
✓ **Legislative**	**and services**	**and services**	**role' to**
❑ Financial laws			**'spokesman**
❑ Employment laws	✓ **New customers**	✓ **New suppliers**	**role'**
❑ National and	**and/or markets**		
international laws			
	✓ **New manage-**		
✓ **Competitive**	**ment**		
and market			
pressures	✓ **Recruitment**		
❑ New markets	**drives**		
❑ New competitors			
❑ New products	✓ **Induction of**		
and services	**new staff**		
❑ Pricing pressures			

This is by no means an exhaustive list, but it is a start!

Identifying the skills needed

Having identified the drivers that create the need for development, you now need to decide just what those needs specifically are.

So let's look at some of these. The following tables, headed External Change, Internal Change, Group Change and Personal Change, list the relevant development needs.

External change

External change	Development needs
✓ **Technological change**	
❑ New plant or machinery (eg where new tools, instruments or appliances are externally developed, which are then installed by your company)	❑ End-user training so that the new kit can be used as fast as possible ❑ Care and maintenance training so that the new kit has as little downtime as possible ❑ Train the trainer so that in-house training can be implemented ❑ Quality standards implementation ❑ Awareness of health and safety issues
❑ New information technology (eg where new software or hardware or updates of existing software and hardware are externally developed, which are then used by your company)	❑ End-user training (at several levels) ❑ System manager training ❑ Help desk training ❑ Care and maintenance training so that the new IT is used as efficiently as possible ❑ Train the trainer so that in-house training can be implemented ❑ User awareness sessions ❑ Quality standards implementation
❑ New methods (eg where new ways of working are developed that will be implemented within your company – for example, new project management methodologies, new financial systems . . .)	❑ Ability to evaluate the usefulness of the new methods ❑ Planning and organisational skills ❑ User awareness sessions ❑ Line manager training for implementing the new systems and implementing quality standards ❑ Documentation skills ❑ End-user training ❑ Awareness of health and safety issues
❑ New infrastructures (eg telephone and communication systems, transport systems and so on, which will materially affect the way your company performs)	❑ Awareness of employment law ❑ User awarness sessions ❑ End-user training

Internal change

Internal change	Development needs
✓ **Reorganisation**	❑ Information sessions
❑ Take-overs	❑ Motivational sessions
❑ Collaboration with other companies	❑ Organisation and logistical skills
	❑ Leadership
❑ Partnerships	❑ Counselling skills
❑ Upsizing	❑ Skills in putting together teams
❑ Downsizing	❑ Project management skills
❑ New premises	❑ ISO design and implementation skills
❑ Implementation of ISO	❑ Understanding of agreements (service-level agreements, roles and responsibilities)
✓ **Introduction of new products and services**	❑ Product training
	❑ Customer handling skills
	❑ Sales training
	❑ Marketing skills
	❑ Support skills
	❑ Pricing skills
	❑ Meetings skills
	❑ Negotiation skills
✓ **New customers and/or markets**	❑ Research skills
	❑ Telephone skills
	❑ Marketing skills
	❑ Sales skills
	❑ Meetings skills
✓ **New management**	❑ Change management
	❑ Motivational skills
	❑ Interpersonal skills
	❑ Assertion training
✓ **Recruitment drives**	❑ Interviewing and selection skills
	❑ Copy writing
	❑ Decision-making skills
	❑ Interpersonal skills
✓ **Induction of new staff**	❑ Knowledge of the company
	❑ Product, service and market knowledge
	❑ Mentoring
	❑ Management skills

Group change

Group change	Development needs
✓ **Redundancy**	❏ CV writing
	❏ Interviewing skills
	❏ Stress management
	❏ Assertion skills
	❏ Counselling skills
	❏ Motivational skills
✓ **Cost-cutting**	❏ Budgeting skills
	❏ Planning skills
	❏ Organisational skills
	❏ Persuasion skills
	❏ Stress management
✓ **Groups amalgamate**	❏ Stress management
	❏ Understanding of teamworking
✓ **New projects**	❏ Project management skills
	❏ Organisational skills
	❏ Networking skills
	❏ Leadership skills
	❏ Meetings skills
✓ **New group members**	❏ Interpersonal skills
	❏ Tasking skills
	❏ Delegation skills
✓ **New suppliers**	❏ Market awareness
	❏ Negotiation skills
	❏ Product awareness
	❏ Interpersonal skills
	❏ Service-level agreement expertise
	❏ Presentation skills

Personal change

Personal change	Development needs
✓ **Promotion**	❑ Specific skills needed for the new job/managerial position
✓ **Job change**	❑ As above
✓ **New tasks**	❑ As above
✓ **Need to delegate**	❑ Delegation skills
	❑ Motivational skills
	❑ Organisational skills
	❑ Interpersonal skills
✓ **New boss**	❑ Assertion skills
✓ **Change from 'backroom role' to 'spokesperson role'**	❑ Presentation skills
	❑ Assertion skills
	❑ Confidence building
	❑ Chairing meetings
	❑ Script writing

Again, I am sure that you will be able to add many more drivers and skills that are absolutely specific to your company and marketplace.

General skills

On top of all of these areas is the need for several basic skills that fall into all the categories: communication, time management, languages, business writing and telephone handling, to name some of them. These are skills that are naturally acquired over the years but may need to be fast-tracked in certain members of your team, particularly where the team members are very young or have little business experience.

Grouping the skills

The skills themselves can now be categorised under three headings: company-specific, business, and individual and personal.

If you go through these lists and identify which skills apply to your team and the company in general, you will have a starting point for your development plan. Obviously there will be needs that apply to the whole team (particularly the company-specific skills) and others that may apply in the future. For example, the business skills set will probably apply to the people who will move from the support roles into line manager and supervisory roles, whereas the personal skills may also apply to everyone at some point to a greater or lesser degree.

Skill categories

Company-specific skills	Business skills	Individual and personal skills
Awareness of:		
❑ Quality standards	❑ Planning and organising	❑ Interpersonal
❑ Company working practices	❑ Risk analysis	❑ Presentation
❑ ISO standards	❑ Market awareness	❑ End-user/technical
❑ Employment law	❑ Customer awareness	❑ Train the trainer
❑ Health and safety	❑ Selling	❑ Evaluation
❑ Legislative changes	❑ Marketing	❑ Stress management
❑ Company knowledge	❑ Product and pricing knowledge	❑ Personal organisation
❑ General customer and market knowledge	❑ Telephone handling	❑ Communication
❑ Company products	❑ Communication	❑ Counselling
❑ Company services	❑ Time management	❑ Physical skills
	❑ Project management	❑ Listening
	❑ Leadership	❑ Questioning
	❑ Decision-making	❑ Assertion
	❑ The ability to analyse problems	❑ Understanding of teamworking
	❑ Written communication	❑ Confidence
	❑ Managing people	❑ Ability to learn
	❑ Delegation	
	❑ Interviewing and selecting	
	❑ Budgeting	

Identifying the people who need developing and areas for development

The next step is to choose who needs developing and which specific skills they need. If you have (and I am sure you do) a complete *and up-to-date* set of job descriptions for every person in your group, then this is not nearly as onerous a task as it might seem.

This is where your knowledge of your team and understanding of its future needs becomes vital. Only you can really know the members of your team and the situations that they are in and are likely to face in the future.

This is where the team's job descriptions and the results of their assessment sessions are needed. (For advice on handling appraisal interviews, Terry Gillen's *The Appraisal Discussion* (CIPD, 1995) is invaluable.)

The job description defines the tasks they have to perform (and inherently the skills needed to perform them). The appraisal interview report covers not only what you perceive they need but, perhaps more importantly, what they perceive they need!

You can now put together an organised list of what you are going to try to achieve with each person in your team – then you can use this to check if there are any gaps between the skills they already have and the skills they are going to need. We are not talking about many years in the future here – think about the coming year. You will probably also discover that some of the skills they have now may require honing or updating.

Here's an example of what the start of such a list might look like:

Example of organised list

Date: 12 July 2000

Name: Jane Reid
Position: Course Administrator

Skills needed: (taken from the job description)		Need/problem	Skills to be developed
Must be able to handle the following systems:			
■ Database	✓		
■ Booking system	✓		
■ Printers, binders and laminators	✓		
■ Diary system	✓		
■ WP package	?	■ Feels the need for more advanced training	■ Advanced WP skills
■ Switchboard	✓		
■ Accounting package	✗	■ User training on new accountancy package	■ Understanding of accountancy practice ■ Actual use of package
Must interact with everyone involved in the training facility, using the following skills:			
■ Telephone handling	✓		
■ E-mail management	✗	■ New system – installed 1/7/2000	■ User training
■ Time management	✓		
■ Handling logistics	✓		
■ Buying/negotiating	✗	■ Never done this before	■ Assertion ■ Buying skills ■ Negotiation skills
■ Handling deliveries	✓		

This is not an arbitrary method; all you need to do is make sure that you have identified:

■ the competencies needed
■ what the background is in terms of what the individual already knows and what he or she is unfamiliar with
■ what skill sets are needed to bring them up to speed.

Do not go any further than this at this stage; the actual planning of the development programme comes later.

When you have looked at the needs of the individual members of your team, go back over your lists and see if there are any common factors. If you identify a skill that they will all need, mark it with a star – this means that everyone needs this skill as a priority. For example, in the list above there is a requirement to be able to use the recently installed e-mail system – this might apply to all members of your staff.

One word of warning about this stage. Many job descriptions do not mention some of the absolutely basic business skills – the ones that are taken for granted like basic numeracy, clarity of speech, ability to fill in forms, pass on messages and so on. Just because they are not mentioned does not mean that they are not vital. As you clambered up the ladder of success you may well have forgotten that once upon a time they had to be learned or refined.

GETTING GOING

'It is best to do things systematically, since we are only human, and disorder is our worst enemy.'
Hesiod, *Works and Days* (eighth century BC)

Now that you have decided who is going to be developed and what they need to be developed in, you can start designing the individual development plans. There is a fail-safe way of going about this:

- prioritising the skills needed for the developee
- setting the timescales
- choosing the most suitable methodologies
- planning the individual training plan
- defining how success is to be measured
- kicking the plan off and monitoring it.

Prioritising the skills

You can prioritise in many ways. Ask yourself these questions:

Importance

Which skills are most important to the developee? Which skills are the most important to the job? For example, the developee may think that his or her most important skill is to be able to write reports, but the job may actually require research and investigative skills, where the reports are written by someone else in the team. Or the developee may consider that leadership skills are essential for the future, but lacks the ability to use the machinery that his or her job depends upon.

Imminence

Which skills are most immediately needed? Is there a new project coming up soon that will require particular skills? For example, the developee may have a long-term need for development in communication skills, but the next project that he or she will be involved with needs skill in risk assessment.

Dependency
Is the developee being held up by a lack of simple skills? Does the developee need to do tasks that are dependent on certain skills? For example, the ability to use a WP package would be dependent on keyboard skills, or the developee may need to learn to use an accountancy package, but may have absolutely no knowledge of accountancy practice or the way accounts are run in your company. In a case like this, it would be necessary to get the developee up to speed on understanding of accountancy before being taught the package.

High/low return on effort
This is a mixture of importance, immediacy and dependency. When the skill is an important one that is needed quickly and where other skills are dependent on it, then this will give a high return on effort. If, however, the skill is not needed quickly, does not affect other skills and is not crucial to the job at the moment, then this would give a low return on effort.

Go back again to the individual development plans (see page 8) and put the development needs into a hierarchy.

Setting timescales
Obviously, the high-priority skills are the ones that need to be tackled first. This means that you need to look at the timescales involved. There are several factors that influence this:

- the time available to the developee – in other words, how much time can the developee take off from his or her day-to-day duties in order to develop the skills needed
- the method or option to be used
- the resources needed for this method or option
- the learning speed and learning preferences of the developee.

High-speed learning tends to be a high-resource business in terms of dedicated learning time (and therefore the need to organise someone to cover the learner's day-to-day tasks), costs and personnel (the experts, trainers, colleagues or mentors that will need to be involved).

Below is a list of possible options with timescales and resources (each methodology is covered in greater depth in Section 3).

Methodology, timescales and resources needed

Methodology	Timescales Fast = a few days Medium = a few weeks	Resources needed (in terms of you or your team's involvement)
Audio tapes/CDs	Fast	Medium
Best practice groups	Medium	Medium
Case studies	Fast	Low
Coaching	Fast	High
Company roadshows	Fast	High
Competitions	Fast/Medium	High
Computer-based training	Fast/Medium	Low
Delegation	Medium	High (at the start)
Demonstration	Fast	High
Feedback	Fast	High
Find the expert	Fast	High
Formal training courses	Fast	High
Group learning	Fast	High
Immersion	Medium	Low
Induction training	Fast	High
Internet/e-learning	Fast/Medium	Low
Job swapping	Fast/Medium	Low
Learning by walking about	Medium	Low
Manuals/reference books	Medium	Low
Mentoring	Fast/Medium	High
Public/private bodies	Medium	Low
Quality circles	Medium	High
Role play	Fast	High
Shadowing	Fast/Medium	Low/Medium
Sit by Nellie	Fast/Medium	Low/Medium
Supplier training	Fast	Low
Teach it back	Fast	Low
Videos/films	Fast/Medium	Low
Video feedback	Fast	Low

Choosing suitable options

Not all options are suitable for all subjects or all learners. You need to consider this when planning.

First let's look at the three types of skills needed:

- **physical skills** – skills that require dexterity, orderly execution, health and safety considerations, quality standards; any skills that require the developee to handle machinery
- **behavioural skills** – skills that are used when interacting with, managing, leading or supporting the team; also communication and motivational skills
- **knowledge-based skills** – skills that are based on the individual's information base, knowledge and ability to plan, evaluate and report.

Now you need to marry up the skills needed with the most suitable options – see the table on page 15.

The programme is nearly together now; the only thing missing is to tailor the skill, the timescale and the method to the learning preference of the developee. We all have our own preferences in the way we take information in and choosing a method that seems the best way to ourselves may not reflect the way the developee likes to learn. For example – you may love reading and find it difficult to understand that other people really do not find reading a pleasure. You need an investigation session to find out how the developee in question prefers to learn.

Introduce the session by finding out how they like to spend their leisure time, then ask them to think back over the past few years about the new skills that they have acquired. These new skills could fall into several categories – simple tasks, hobbies and pastimes, business skills.

Skills and methodologies

Type of skill	Suitable methodologies
Physical skills	■ Coaching
	■ Competitions
	■ Computer-based training
	■ Delegation
	■ Demonstration
	■ Feedback
	■ Formal training courses
	■ Immersion
	■ Manuals/reference books
	■ Quality groups
	■ Shadowing
	■ Sit by Nellie
	■ Supplier training
	■ Teach it back
	■ Videos/films
Behavioural skills	■ Case studies
	■ Coaching
	■ Delegation
	■ Feedback
	■ Find the expert
	■ Formal training courses
	■ Group learning
	■ Job swapping
	■ Mentoring
	■ Role play
	■ Shadowing
	■ Sit by Nellie
	■ Videos/films
	■ Video feedback
Knowledge-based skills	■ Audio tapes/CDs
	■ Case studies
	■ Competitions
	■ Computer-based training
	■ Formal training courses
	■ Group learning
	■ Immersion
	■ Induction training
	■ Internet/e-learning
	■ Job swapping
	■ Learning by walking about
	■ Manuals/reference books
	■ Mentoring
	■ Public/private bodies
	■ Roadshows
	■ Quality circles
	■ Teach it back

Here are the types of question you could ask them:

Set 1 How do they like to spend their leisure time?

A	B	C
❑ Reading, listening to music, TV, radio	❑ Physical activities	❑ Group activities

Set 2 Learning simple tasks (things like learning to use household equipment, using new tools etc)

How did they approach the task?

A	B	C
❑ Made a plan	❑ Went ahead with no planning	❑ Asked for advice

What did they use to help them?

A	B	C
❑ Reading matter or reference matter	❑ Trial and error	❑ Found an expert

How did they consolidate their learning?

A	B	C
❑ Scheduled regular practice sessions	❑ Improved by doing	❑ Asked someone to test them or check what they had done

How did they refine those skills?

A	B	C
❑ Set incremental goals	❑ Just kept on doing	❑ Discussed progress with others

Set 3 Hobbies and pastimes (like sports, music, model making, collecting)

How do they find out more about the hobby or pastime?

A	B	C
❑ Books, reference matter	❑ By doing it	❑ Clubs, friends

How often do they spend time on their hobby?

A	B	C
❑ Regularly	❑ Spasmodically	❑ When there's a meeting

Have they taken any courses or qualifications in the hobby or pastime?

A	B	C
❏ Yes or intend to	❏ No	❏ Not unless the group wants to

Set 4 Business skills (MBA, professional qualifications, IT skills, handling new equipment/procedures etc)

Why did they learn the new skill?

A	B	C
❏ Part of a personal development plan	❏ It just happened	❏ Peer pressure or the need to keep up with the group

How did they learn it?

A	B	C
❏ By themselves or from reference material	❏ By doing it	❏ By asking others, having a mentor, discussion

How did they refine or develop the new skill?

A	B	C
❏ Conscious practice, reading and research	❏ By doing it	❏ Help from friends

Interpreting the results

It is highly likely that there will be more than one answer for each question (very few people have only one way of learning), so probe for preferences. If no pattern emerges (a fairly even spread of As, Bs and Cs), then they would be comfortable with any of the options mentioned here. This is what is most likely to happen – it is dangerous to pigeonhole people. What might be a preference in one situation might seem totally inappropriate in another. However, if a pattern emerges then look at the table on page 19, which gives you an idea of the most comfortable ways of developing themselves for the As, Bs and Cs.

*A*s like to research things well, have a clear pattern to the learning process, like to do things step by step, are happy with reference material and are self-motivated. They need reassurance that they are reaching the required standards, so watch over them! They often have very high personal standards and can be hypercritical of themselves. They are often not happy with experimentation or sink-or-swim situations and have a cautious and sometimes timid approach to new skills. They have a long attention span and often get completely immersed in what they are doing. They are happiest when working and researching alone, and while this can be very effective it does not give them the chance to discuss and so refine their new knowledge.

Bs like to get on with things. They want to do it for themselves and usually have the confidence to try! They are not happy learning from the printed page or screen. You will need to keep a weather eye out for them in case they get into bad habits, since they usually find their own way of doing things (which may or may not be according to laid-down procedures). They become easily bored with repetitive tasks and activities that take a long time to give a payback. When in doubt they often guess the answer rather than refer to a manual or ask for help. They like working with others and can be easily distracted by others or tasks that seem more exciting. They learn fast and usually effectively, but will often try to bend the rules to get a faster result.

Cs learn best when they can talk about what is happening and watch how others do things. They may be comfortable with learning alone, but they definitely need to discuss and clarify before they can refine their skills. They think holistically and like to know how everything fits together and what the background is to any new information. They are usually logical and will question anything that seems arbitrary or sloppily expressed. They are often intellectually experimental and will try to find other ways of performing or integrating tasks.

See the table on page 19 for an illustration of how these types work differently.

Learning types and methodologies

Methodology	A Organised, disciplined, orderly, works well alone, likes reading	B Confident, happy-go-lucky, not keen on reading, likes activity	C Works well in groups, needs discussion
Audio tapes/CDs	✔		✔
Best practice groups	✔	✔	✔
Case studies	✔	✔	✔
Coaching	✔	✔	✔
Company roadshows	✔	✔	✔
Competitions	✔	✔	✔
Computer-based training	✔		
Delegation	✔	✔	✔
Demonstration	✔		✔
Feedback	✔	✔	✔
Find the expert	✔		✔
Formal training courses	✔		✔
Group learning		✔	✔
Immersion		✔	
Induction training	✔	✔	✔
Internet/e-learning	✔		
Job swapping	✔	✔	✔
Learning by walking about	✔	✔	✔
Manuals/reference books	✔		
Mentoring	✔	✔	✔
Public/private bodies	✔		✔
Quality circles	✔	✔	✔
Role play		✔	✔
Shadowing	✔	✔	✔
Sit by Nellie	✔	✔	✔
Supplier training	✔	✔	✔
Teach it back		✔	✔
Videos/films	✔		
Video feedback	✔	✔	✔

Drawing everything together

So you know and have prioritised which skills need to be developed, and who needs developing. You have investigated the way each of your people likes to learn and looked at the options available to you.

Now you can draw up the actual development schedule. Here are a couple of examples:

Example 1

Felicity Ffarnes-Barnes is a new hire. She has an NVQ in business administration and this is her first job. She has been in the company for six months. At her job evaluation interview you and she agreed on her development needs (see table opposite). She is self-motivated and very sporty, she works particularly well with groups and is highly gregarious. She has made strong friendships with the people she works with and is not afraid to ask for help. She does not like sitting still for long and confesses that reading bores her. You know that she learns fast because she has fitted into the job well and seems to cope with whatever gets thrown at her. She enjoyed the induction course that she attended on the week she joined the company. Her development plan is shown on page 21.

Example 2

Nigel Barrymore-Ferrars is an extremely competent senior lathe operator. He has been doing the job for six years and has steadily risen to be the most competent operator you have out of a team of four. He is orderly and meticulous in his work and often offers to help others out when they are having difficulties. You are about to employ another two operators and want Nigel to become the team leader.

At his job evaluation interview you identified his development needs. Nigel is a real mixture of learning types – he loves collecting information and has a large library at home and he reads voraciously. He also belongs to several societies and

Development Plan 1

Name: Felicity Ffarnes-Barnes
Position: Course Administrator
Date: 16 July 2000

Development need	Timescale	Methodology
To be able to use WP package to an advanced level	Quickly – within two weeks	Sit by Nellie Coaching Demonstration Find the expert Immersion
To be able to use accountancy package	Within the next four months	Coaching Find the expert
To be able to use new e-mail system	ASAP (for the whole group too)	Coaching Teach it back
Buying skills	Within the next six months	Find the expert Shadowing
Negotiation skills	Within the next six months	Coaching Sit by Nellie Shadowing Role play
Assertion skills	Within the next six months	Mentoring Role play

is hoping to take an Open University Degree in two years' time. He is a leading light at the local darts club and has a wide circle of friends, both inside and outside work. His development plan is shown on page 22.

Creating the individual development plan

At this point there are several considerations.

Who needs to be involved (as well as the developee)?

The more involved the developee is in his or her programme, the more commitment he or she will make to it. This planning stage should always be a joint effort. What you, as manager, can do is to ease the way – after all, you probably have many more contacts than the developee and the seniority to make decisions about how your team spend their time. You may also have to negotiate with other managers to free up some of their people's time when necessary. This is often a case of 'quid pro quo', as your team may be able to help their people as well. Make sure that you do not overburden individual members of your team and keep a tally of how much time you have used up from other teams and sources.

Development Plan 2

Name: Nigel Barrymore-Ferrars
Position: Senior Lathe Operator (Engineering Team Leader in 3 months)
Date: 16 July 2000

Development need	Timescale	Methodology
Leadership skills	ASAP	Coaching
		Formal training when it becomes available
		Mentoring
		Reference material
		Shadowing
		Videos/films
Reporting practices and skills	Within two months	Any reference material
		Coaching
		LBWA
		Quality circles
		Shadowing
Delegation skills	Within four months	Mentoring
		Role play
Training skills	Within six months	Coaching
		Demonstration
		Find the expert
		Teach it back
		Video feedback
Health and safety delivery	Within three months	CBT
		Public/private bodies
		Reference material
		Videos/films
Assertion	Within nine months	Group learning
		Mentoring
		Role play
Employment practices (line management responsibilities and the way your company handles these)	ASAP	Case studies
		Delegation
		Find the expert
		Job swapping
		Reference material/ manuals

Where to find reference material

This should be part of the learning curve for the developee. Over the years you and your team will build up a comprehensive package of reference material and so should make space for this. It is extremely useful to keep an up-to-date list of the material available – and be ruthless about getting rid of out-of-date material. Obsolescent reference material is worse than useless.

What *(if any)* dedicated space is needed?

In my experience there are never enough meeting rooms when you need them, let alone quiet spaces where people can work uninterrupted. This is where you can really help your people by making sure that space is made available on a regular basis.

You can now add the resources needed to the programme plan.

On page 24 you can see Felicity's completed programme plan.

Defining how success is to be measured

Before the developee starts the programme, it is most important that clear goals are defined and set. Without goals neither of you can know whether progress is being made. Again, the developee should be involved in setting these goals. Make the goals incremental, that is, in stages rather than an overarching target that might take months to reach. For example, supposing the developee wants to become skilled at word processing, ask him or her to sit down and define the stages that he or she will have to go through in order to feel competent. One way the developee could start to do this is by watching someone who is already competent. Out of that session might come a list like this:

- learn how to switch on, log on and access the package
- learn how to input text
- learn how to format text

■ learn how to print text
■ learn how to make tables and alphabetical lists
■ learn how to back up the data

and so on and so on . . .

Working from a checklist like this keeps the developee on track and progressing.

Completed Programme Plan

Name: Felicity Ffarnes-Barnes
Position: Course Administrator
Date: 16 July 2000–January 2001

Development need	Methodology	Resources needed
To be able to use WP package to an advanced level Timescale: quickly – within two weeks	■ Sit by Nellie ■ Coaching ■ Demonstration ■ Immersion ■ Find the expert	■ Name Nellie ■ Name coach ■ Name demonstrator ■ Set tasks ■ Help-desk?
To be able to use accountancy package. Timescale: within the next four months	■ Coaching ■ Find the expert	■ Name coach ■ Introduce XX from financial division
To be able to use new e-mail system Timescale: ASAP (for the whole group too)	■ Coaching ■ Teach it back	■ Ask someone from IT support department ■ Felicity to give demonstration to group within a fortnight
Buying skills Timescale: within the next six months	■ Find the expert ■ Shadowing	■ Ask XX from purchasing to help ■ Felicity to spend the day with purchasing
Negotiation skills Timescale: within the next six months	■ Coaching ■ Sit by Nellie ■ Shadowing ■ Role play	■ Ask XX from sales to organise this (brief him first)
Assertion skills Timescale: within the next six months	■ Mentoring ■ Role play	■ Appoint XX as mentor (brief her first) to organise this

Some measurements of new skills are almost self-evident – you can observe the person being developed actually doing the job effectively. This applies particularly to physical skills and some behavioural skills. Other developing skills need to be examined more carefully – knowledge-based and some behavioural skills are harder to observe in action unless you have a plan worked out in advance. What is paramount is that the developee receives and gives regular feedback (see Section 3, page 60). The easiest way is to have a debrief immediately (or as soon as possible) after the newly learned skill has been used.

Persuading and motivating the developee

Developing new skills is one of the most motivational activities that you can provide for your people. One of the nicer realities of working with people is their readiness to develop and be developed. Everyone likes to be adept at what they are doing and looks forward to gaining new skills and capabilities, and most people are genuinely interested in learning more about their job.

It is always best to avoid the deadly 'mandatory' label. I have found that people who feel that they are forced to undertake new learning activities simply find excuses to put them off. This will lead to time and effort on your part in persuading them. It is much better to spend that time up front by jointly putting together the development plan, so that it is as much their plan as yours. If the developee does not know why the new skill is needed, what the new skill entails, what the timescales are, what the rewards will be and that you are firmly behind them, then he or she will prevaricate, shilly shally and find every excuse under the sun just to carry on without any changes.

Do

- look closely at people's preferences in the way they take in new information
- show them exactly how useful the new skills will be

- involve them in the planning process
- ensure that they value any formal rewards they might receive
- keep on showing that you appreciate the time they are spending on the development activities
- make sure that any resources they need are available or that funds exist to get them
- set reasonable timescales
- give specific and timely feedback on their increasing skill and knowledge set.

Don't

- force them to work in ways that they find uncomfortable
- make the development activity mandatory with associated penalties for missing it out
- assume that they can get on without any help
- specify unbendable rules about the way they use their new skills – let them work out the way that makes them most efficient
- criticise or carp if they do not develop fast enough – check that they are getting the help and resources they need.

That said, there are situations where people are reluctant to start development activities and others where they lose heart part way through the programme.

Reluctance to start

They are not confident that they are capable of actually gaining the skill. This is particularly true of people who have been working successfully for years with one set of skills and believe that you cannot teach an old dog new tricks (or that this particular old dog cannot learn any new tricks). The secret here is to do some heavy confidence-building and link the old skills to the new. This was very common in the early 1980s when computer skills were becoming more and more necessary. PAs and secretaries were sent on courses because they simply would not try to learn for themselves. They were genuinely afraid of the apparent speed and complexity of the technology and its (to them) amazing capacity for crashing, erasing, fouling up and sabotaging their work. This was not helped by the extremely technical language that surrounded the new kit and the massive (and often unusable) user documentation that came with it. When working with these sorts of fears, it is necessary to stress what is the *same* (typing skill, layout etc) rather than what is very different. Reassurance was the order of the day rather than daring flights into the unknown.

There have been so many changes lately that they are shell-shocked and really need to consolidate these changes before they try anything new. It is very tiring to adapt to constant change. Not just physically, but mentally. When your team of people are in a state of flux, do not expect them to take on new skills; wait until the situation has become more comfortable and then start the programme.

They genuinely believe that they are very good at a particular skill and take offence at the suggestion that they need to improve it. This is a tough one, calling for diplomacy and tact. Stress that the old skills are still valuable, that they are not going to be thrown away or forgotten, but will act as the basis of even greater skills. Again, any suggestion that the development is your choice for them, rather than their personal choice, should be avoided.

They are really overworked and become panicky at the thought of yet another set of tasks. This is somewhat like the constant change problem. If they are absolutely at the edge of their energy levels, then it is no use adding to their burdens – the whole lot will suffer. On the other hand, a more efficient way of working may well make the other tasks easier and more efficient. As an illustration, take this case of a massive office move – everyone needed to pack up and rationalise their working space, tools and filing, and this all had to be done in a fairly short time. The team manager noted that in the development plan of the office co-ordinator's team there was a great need for filing and logistical skills. There was one really experienced office manager in the team, so they put together a small project team, involving the people who needed those skills and the person who had them and between them planned how the move would go – well in advance. The result was a highly successful move and the transfer of the necessary skills at the very time that they were needed.

They have a hidden agenda that you do not know about. Hidden agendas are the bear traps of management. Take this scenario: a 45-year-old line manager in a hard-pressed and newly rationalised purchasing department was obviously having difficulties handling her new responsibilities, among which were the need to use a computer for herself (rather than having a secretary) and the need to delegate to and communicate more effectively with her people. These needs were freely admitted and her difficulties were having a very adverse effect on the productivity of her team. A development programme was put in place involving finding experts, mentoring and feedback sessions – and still nothing happened – she 'forgot' to attend feedback sessions, she 'was too busy' to go to meetings or discussions with the experts, she would not return her mentors' calls. What was going on? Her manager was flummoxed until she heard on the grapevine that the line manager was hoping for redundancy and simply did not see the need to develop at all (and possibly hoping that the very lack of skills that had been identified would lead to this). So – the secret here is to look at as many of the facts available to you – including those that may seem outside the actual job and role itself.

Losing heart part way through
Lack of effective feedback
Regular feedback (see page 60) keeps the learning curve growing. This feedback is not so much a checking exercise but a

boosting session where the developee is given encouragement and the chance to sort out any problems.

The new skills are not being used enough

New skills are easily forgotten unless they are used. There is little point in spending valuable time learning to do, say, presentations, if the opportunity to practise and refine those skills is not there. As manager, make sure that the opportunity to use these skills is provided.

The pace is too fast

This may apply particularly to the As, who very often like to take their time making sure that they thoroughly understand new tasks and skills before hurling themselves into them.

The pace is too slow

This may apply particularly to the Bs, who get easily bored. Break the modules up into shorter units and feed back to them more often.

Work gets in the way

Your job as a manager is to help them to prioritise their workload. They may not feel that they have the authority to put certain tasks aside or may feel that the development activity is not particularly pressing or important. Keep in touch with them and keep stressing the usefulness of the new skills they are gaining.

Whatever the problem, do not lose heart – if you regularly discuss their progress with them, this in itself is a motivational factor

Kicking the programme off

Just as every book, film and play has a definite start and end, so should a development module. There is (and quite rightly too) a trend towards the 'constantly learning organisation'. But this does not mean that new sections of a long-term and ongoing programme should be allowed to start or end without some sort of fanfare. You could use your group meetings as a forum where each group member updates the rest on what he or she is undertaking in terms of development. This also allows the rest of the group to offer their own expertise to the developee. You could have a CV or job description updating session where you add the new skills to the existing ones. You could add the developee's name to your database of experts (see 'Find the Expert' page 64). Whatever you do, make sure that each learning and development activity is clearly noted and rewarded; it will pay large dividends in motivational terms.

So now, on to the options themselves. Section 3 shows you the choices available to you. It is by no means exhaustive, but will give you a kickstart.

THE DEVELOPMENT CHOICES – METHODS FOR DEVELOPING YOUR TEAM

Alphabetical list of options

- audio tapes/CDs
- best practice groups
- case studies
- coaching
- company roadshows
- competitions
- computer-based training (CBT)
- delegation
- demonstration
- feedback
- find the expert
- formal training courses
- group learning
- immersion
- induction training
- Internet/e-learning
- intranet
- job swapping
- learning by walking about
- manuals/reference books
- mentoring
- public/private bodies
- quality circles
- role play
- shadowing
- sit by Nellie
- supplier training
- teach it back
- video feedback
- videos/films.

You have a myriad options for developing your people. These are some of them, ranging from very simple (sit by Nellie), up to highly sophisticated 'learning plans' where you map out a series of linked exercises, experiences and activities that may well extend over a considerable period and require considerable effort from you as a manager.

However, all of these methods and activities will involve, at the very least, some basic input from you. At the start you must identify the developee's need, choose the best options and consider the mindset of the person you are developing. After the exercise or activity, you need to check that learning has taken place and then look at the next step.

In order to help you choose which options and methods would be best for your individual 'developees', this section has been laid out as follows:

- option
- a table showing the pros and cons and where this particular option is most suitable
- finding help
- setting it up
- does it work? – how to check whether learning has happened
- more activities (cross-referenced)
- hints and tips.

The section ends with some suggestions of ways you can mix and match these options.

Audio tapes/CDs

These are highly portable, easily made and extremely useful when information needs to be quickly assimilated. It is also an excellent method for learning new languages and particularly beneficial for employees who spend time travelling. I have seen this used to great effect by a large IT company who used audio tapes to keep its highly mobile sales force up to date on company news and products. It also used it to reinforce negotiation and selling techniques, sales processes and market information, which were covered on more formal training courses. Interestingly, the tapes were produced in house, by the sales, support and marketing teams themselves, which was a process that developed the teams' knowledge and communication skills no end.

For	Against
■ highly portable	■ not everyone is completely
■ not expensive (if created	happy learning through the
in house)	spoken word only.
■ easily updatable	
■ a developmental opportunity	
for those who create the tapes.	

Finding help

Provided that you do not need a highly professional result with music and sound effects, these can be easily produced in house. If you are aiming for something more glitzy, then there are many audio tape production companies who will not only script and produce the tapes with background music and special effects, but will also find professional performers for the recording session and do the duplication and sleeving for you. This then becomes considerably more expensive than the DIY version. There are also scores of companies producing training tapes on all subjects, from sales skills to accountancy practices.

Whichever you use, the most important factor is the quality of the information – if you are sourcing this from within your company, there is a need for a 'co-ordinating editor' who understands what needs to be included and how the information is to be interpreted. I have found that marketing and product departments are particularly good at this.

Setting it up

- ■ Put together a production team.
- ■ Decide on the scope of the tapes and what you want them to achieve.

■ Break the information into modular packages, no more than 10–15 minutes each (more than this and the listener's attention will wander).
■ Reinforce the learning with repetition and quizzes.
■ Make the recording.
■ Duplicate it and sleeve it.
■ Distribute the tapes.

Resources and people needed

■ a co-ordinating editor who will be responsible for the content of the finished tapes
■ scriptwriters and performers (you could put a team of people together for this)
■ recording and duplicating equipment
■ labelling for the finished tapes
■ a method of distributing the tapes.

Checking on learning

Include a questionnaire in the tape/sleeve that will give you feedback on the usefulness (or otherwise) of the tape and ask for suggestions for future tapes.

Similar activities

SEE *VIDEOS/FILMS* ON PAGE 98

Hints and tips

■ Keep the modules on the tapes relatively short. Certainly there are few people who will listen really attentively for more than 15 minutes at a stretch.
■ Use humour and an informal approach to make the information interesting and pleasurable to listen to.
■ Ruthlessly dispose of out-of-date tapes.

34

Best practice groups

These were extensively used in manufacturing plants to increase productivity and throughput. They are also very useful for developing your team in the basic and essential business skills that every team member needs. Best practice refers to the definition of the optimum ways of working and is continually revised as business processes, technology and the infrastructure of commerce change.

For	Against
■ develop good business skills by examining and refining the way you currently do business ■ not expensive ■ not only does the group learn about best practice, but their findings lead to better productivity.	■ there is sometimes a reluctance to change established patterns of working (the sometimes negative impact of change is, however, greatly reduced if the team members are actively involved in defining the changes).

Finding help

The more experienced the group members, the more they will bring to the exercise. Inexperienced members will bring a new eye to the problem. If you set the best practice group up with enthusiasm and communicate the validity of what they are doing they will join in with gusto.

Setting it up

■ Form a group of three to six people (fewer and there is not enough input, more and there are too many for each to contribute effectively).

■ Ask them to rotate the leadership around the group for each meeting.

■ Give them the topic or ask them to decide which aspect of group working they are going to examine.

■ As a group they decide how they are going to examine the aspect chosen. For example, a group from the help desk team at a large manufacturer may decide that they want to look at the complaints procedures that they are currently using. As a starting point they need to look at how complaints are handled at the moment, followed by suggestions as to how this may be improved, followed by a planning session leading to an implementation plan and action lists.

Resources and people needed

■ time and space for the meetings.

Checking on learning
Look at the results!

Similar activities
SEE *QUALITY CIRCLES* ON PAGE 85

Hints and tips

■ The groups should report back regularly, both to you and the rest of the team.
■ Their suggestions should be actioned. If there is no outcome from the best practice group meetings, the members of the group will begin to think that it is just a talking shop and will lose motivation to really try to solve the problems.

Case studies

This involves learning from others' experience. A case study is a history of effective (or ineffective) business activities that is used as a basis for discussion, analysis and problem-solving. The areas covered can range from management skills to marketing plans, from new product introduction to company restructuring. Examples can be found in professional journals, trade magazines, business books, television and radio programmes and electronic publications – in fact any source that looks in depth at the ways business works. You can create your own case studies using examples of either absolutely splendid or appallingly inept activities that have occurred in your own company (though be careful not to name names in the case of the appalling ones!).

For	Against
■ easy to collect examples	■ must be kept up to date
■ no significant cost	■ be careful when using case studies from your own company that you do not hold anyone up to ridicule.
■ uses real-life issues in a safe environment	
■ can be used by developees with a wide range of skills.	

Finding help

Start with any training courses you have attended that have used case studies – these will be (or should be!) carefully constructed. Go to your local library and search the business section. Talk to your colleagues – they will all have war stories that can act as a base for learning. One valuable source of ready-made case studies is the CIPD Case Studies Club (www.cipd.co.uk/casestudies/).

Setting it up

Select your case study and decide what it is that it illustrates. For example, take the fictional case study on pages 38–40, which was used as a project management development exercise:

PROJECT MANAGEMENT SKILLS CASE STUDY

SUPERPAK EQUIPMENT RELOCATION

PHASE 1

Following recent meetings between product line management and the Superpak technical services department, you have been nominated as team leader of the Superpak Equipment Relocation Project.

On the basis of the enclosed documentation, you are asked as a first step to specify the product objectives.

Enclosed:
- Superpak memo dated 1 March 2001

SUPERPAK MEMO   Superpak Packaging Inc
                                              2 Sneinton Lane
                                              Sherwood
                                              Berkshire SI47 2DD

To: Technical Services Vice-President
From: Superpak Executive Vice-President   1 March 2001

Subject: **Superpak Equipment Relocation (Sneinton Lane)**

The Superpak Product Line is projecting the purchase of a used, fully depreciated assembly line from the recently shut down Sneinton Lane plant (UK) to replace the Superpak Line in Perma, Malaysia.

Background

The assembly line at Perma currently manufactures: (1) bubble-wrap sheeting, and, (2) plastic-fibre packing.

Possible justification

Recently the success of Superpak PVC-free packaging materials in the Pacific Rim markets called for a reassessment of production capacity. Current plans indicate a shortage towards the end of 2001 and despite the introduction of five shift operations (seven days/week), virtually no spare capacity will be available to satisfy a high demand should the forecasts be too conservative. Additional production capacity would enable the Perma Plant to become a regular supplier of the Pacific Rim branches of Superpak (they currently import from Superpak Australia). The new production facilities are planned to be available during the first quarter of 2002. Significant quality improvement would be achieved with the proposed Superpak Sneinton Lane equipment.

Other information

Similar equipment exists in the Superpak Plant located in Singapore. Superpak UK is forecasting the relocation of several pieces of the Sneinton Lane equipment into other facilities. Other Superpak operations are interested in acquiring the Sneinton Lane assembly line.

Mechanical and electrical adaptation costs will be incurred in addition to the relocation costs. On a recent installation of similar equipment in Singapore, installation costs amounted to approximately US$1 million.

The following people must be involved:

Superpak USA	–	Director of Central Engineering
Superpak (Sing.)	–	Packaging Technical Centre
		Director of Manufacturing
		Plant Manager
		Process Engineer

Timing

A technical feasibility study including a cost estimate for the relocation in Perma, Malaysia, must be completed by May 2002. If there is an economic justification, the new line should be on stream by the first quarter of 2003.

(This sort of case study could be used for the following activities:

- creating a project justification document
- defining project statements and stakeholder lists
- project planning
- risk analysis . . . and a multitude of other processes.)

- Give out the case study to the developees involved at least a week before the first session.
- A minimum of two hours should be set aside for each session – the length of the entire exercise will depend on the complexity of the case study.
- Gather the developees together with as many experts as you can rustle up.
- Have the topics that you are going to discuss written up where everyone can see them.
- Start with a general overview of the case study (keeping the chosen topics in mind and stressing the relevance of the case study to the actual tasks they will be attempting in the real-life situation).
- Assign tasks, explaining exactly what is needed. (For example, one of the tasks from the case study set out above might be to produce a project objectives statement. In this case you would need a blank justification document for them to work on. You can see one at the top of the next page.)

RELOCATION PROJECT JUSTIFICATION DOCUMENT

Title: *Superpak Equipment Relocation to Perma, Malaysia*
Objective:
Justification:
Scope:
Project Leader:
Team:
Date: *Today's date*

- When they have completed the task, debrief on their success or otherwise (it is useful to have any actual documentation from the case study available for comparison).
- When the case study session is complete, ask them what they have learned and how they will use this information.

Resources and people needed

- the case study documentation and a set of topics to work on
- space and time to hold the case study sessions.

Checking on learning
Feedback from the sessions should give you a good idea of how people are developing, but the real proof of the pudding will be in the way they perform when they undertake the same sort of task in real life.

Similar activities

- discussion groups.

Hints and tips

- If at all possible, have access to people who know the details of the case study (if you are using a case study from your own company, the original participants may still be available). If you have taken the case study from a source outside your own company, you will need to find experts who can, at the least, make an educated guess at what is likely to have happened.

■ Start with simple case studies and work up to more complex ones – people's skills will grow as they become used to analysing and planning.

Coaching

This is a tried and true method of refining and enhancing individual and team performance (not only, by the way, on the part of the coachee, but also on the part of the coach!). Think of a football coach, an athletics coach, a swimming coach – what the coach essentially does is to set goals and work out a planned series of exercises and activities. These will set up the basis for effective performance and will also gradually increase skill levels. Then there is a debrief on performance with suggestions on how to improve. Above all the coach is there to encourage, encourage, encourage!

The secret of successful coaching lies not only in the skill and experience of the coach but also in his or her ability to communicate the reality of what is being passed on. For this reason it is not enough for the coach to be a star performer; it is also vital that the coach should remember the stages he or she went through when gaining the required skills. To do this the coach needs to take a long-term view of the learning process, using his or her own experience of timescales, setbacks, triumphs and failures. Good coaching is not theory-based; it comes from real knowledge and practice.

For	Against
■ reality-based – works always with what is possible	■ the planning process needs dedication and time.
■ efficiently passes on experience that may never have been written down	
■ leads to a strong bond between the coach and coachee.	

Finding help

Star performers may well make excellent coaches, but there is a need to check their ability to explain things simply without missing out basic steps. The more adept we are, the more likely we are to make assumptions about basic skill levels – for example an experienced machinery operator may take it for granted that the person he or she coaching is *au fait* with simple things like switching on, switching off and taking safety precautions. A star salesman may take it for granted that the person he or she is coaching knows where to obtain information about a company or who to ask about billing and invoicing.

You will also need to make sure that the coach can spare the time, not only for the actual coaching, but also for the planning of the coaching sessions. This is not as easy as it sounds, since star performers are usually out and about performing like stars and will need persuading that the time they spend coaching is as valuable as the time spent fulfilling, or indeed overreaching, their targets!

A really valuable and easily digested book on coaching is *The Manager as Coach and Mentor* by Eric Parsloe (CIPD, 1999).

Setting it up

- Take a careful look at the skills that need to be coached – it may be necessary to break these down into modules (packets of learning specific to a particular need). For example, supposing you wanted to coach someone in telephone selling, you might break the learning modules into:
    - time management (organising the day)
    - product knowledge
    - customer research
    - voice training
    - introducing yourself on the phone
    - defining customer need

- selling skills
- closing the call
- logging and recording the outcomes of the call
- following up the call.

You might well find someone who is excellent at all of these things, but it is more likely that you would need a mixture of people (in this case you might need someone to coach the logistics, someone to cover product, someone else for selling skills and so on).

- Meet with the coach and the coachee(s) and thrash out the programme together. This might take the form of a set of working sessions where they all get together and cover one module at a time.
- Decide which basic skills need reinforcing at each session (in the case of teleselling perhaps these might be scheduling, customer research and voice training).
- Make a timetable for the sessions – coaching is incremental learning and should take place regularly.
- Agree how you will measure the success of the sessions.

Resources and people needed

- dedicated time for the coaching sessions (on both sides)
- there is no particular need for a dedicated 'coaching space'; the best coaching takes place at the coalface.

Checking on learning

- regular reports
- feedback on sales
- feedback from the coach
- feedback on productivity.

Similar activities

A coaching session may use many of the methodologies mentioned here:

> SEE *CASE STUDIES* ON PAGE 36; *DELEGATION* ON PAGE 53; *FEEDBACK* ON PAGE 60; *FIND THE EXPERT* ON PAGE 64; *GROUP LEARNING* ON PAGE 67; *MENTORING* ON PAGE 82; *QUALITY CIRCLES* ON PAGE 85; *ROLE PLAY* ON PAGE 87

Hints and tips

- Make sure that the coach fully understands the importance of his or her role. Very often the targets that are set for the high flyers within a company (who of course are the ones you want as coaches) can make coaching sessions seem like an interruption to their working life. It is understandable that if they are targeted on 'doing' rather than coaching there is a conflict of interest. You will probably need to involve the coach's manager in motivating him or her.
- You will need to give encouragement and praise to both parties.

Company roadshows

This is a method that I have seen used to great advantage in a large IT company that was developing its portfolio of products and services at a great rate. Once every year or so it held an in-house roadshow where every division (including HR, legal, financial and all other infrastructure departments) had a 'market stall' where they explained exactly what they did, what they provided and how they did it. Everyone working for the company was encouraged to attend. The 'stallholders' offered all sorts of inducements ranging from T-shirts to luncheon vouchers to the people who passed through their 'stalls', with quizzes and tests that gave small prizes for correct answers. Customers who happened to be in the building were also encouraged to visit. The buzz was palpable and the comments overheard later were very positive. In terms of passing on product knowledge it proved to be very successful, but possibly of even more use was the increased awareness of the business processes involved in running the company and the links between the departments.

For	Against
■ allow the 'exhibitors' to practise their presentations	■ can be expensive and time-consuming
■ give an overview of the company that is bang up to date	■ need 'selling' hard.
■ lead to good networking within the company	
■ allows specialists to understand where they fit into the company.	

Finding help

This is a company-wide exercise; each department sets up its own exhibition. There needs to be an overall project manager. Often this exercise can be added to a commercial exhibition.

Setting it up

■ Set up a project team with members from each of the departments involved.

■ Typically allow two to four months for preparation.

■ Publicise the event widely – since all departments are involved there is usually high interest.

■ Collect together all the reference material needed.

■ Organise the quizzes and prizes.

■ Run the event.

Resources and people needed

■ time and effort

■ a large enough space (although departments may choose to site their stalls actually within the space they work).

Checking on learning
The prizes and handouts are only awarded when the knowledge of the visitors to the stall has been checked.

Similar activities
You could run a cut-down version of the company roadshow where each department holds an open day, coffee morning or working lunch; although these are on a smaller scale, the learning and networking would be just as effective. Other similar activities include:

- trade shows
- exhibitions.

SEE *INDUCTION TRAINING* ON PAGE 71

Hints and tips
Draw up a list of what you want to find out about and why (for example, company procedures and products, how other departments service their clients, how they do their advertising, customer attitudes etc) and concentrate on these. Having no particular agenda leads to a tendency to wander about and not evaluate what you are seeing.

Competitions

For many people, learning by competition is a quick and effective way of gaining information; the competitive spirit also leads to an enthusiastic approach, as well as fostering team bonding. It is also an opportunity for the people within the team to share their knowledge and experience. One company I worked with had a six-monthly competition for its marketing groups where the winning group was the one who could collect the most information on their competitors (they divided the information into several categories: hardware, services, aftercare, reliability, future products and so on). The prize was a weekend away of their choice with the partner of their choice for each team member. The result was not only a brilliant database of competitive information for marketing, but also involvement from most of the rest of the company. The competing teams roamed around the company collecting information not only from sales and pre-sales, but also from the product management group, the help desks, and, as far as we could see, everyone they came across – including the regulars in the local pub.

For	Against
■ relatively inexpensive ■ extensive knowledge sharing ■ fosters good teamworking.	■ care needs to be taken that the competition doesn't overshadow normal working (particularly with very competitive individuals).

Finding help

You will need an organiser – there needs to be a central point for setting the competition up and deciding who will win. You could put a team together to decide the rules and terms of engagement.

Setting it up

- Set up the competition goals. Here are some ideas:
  - a searching exercise to identify every single stage in one of your business processes (who, what, where and when)
  - a competition to contact as many customers as possible within a short timescale
  - a race to assemble/disassemble a particular piece of kit
  - a timed scavenger hunt to find as many pieces of company literature about a particular subject as possible
  - a treasure hunt to find and identify a specified list of essential business equipment (photocopiers, faxes, printers and so on); this sort of 'inventory' game is particularly useful during induction courses.
- Formulate the competition rules.

- Set a timescale.
- Decide on the prize (make this meaningful and worthwhile for the competitors – certificates are not always as motivational as their designers think they are).
- Post the rules, accept entries, kick the competition off.

Resources and people needed

- time and effort on the part of the organisers
- the prizes
- prior communication with anyone who might be involved.

Checking on learning

Judging the competition will show who has learned what.

Similar activities

SEE *COMPANY ROADSHOWS* ON PAGE 47; *INDUCTION TRAINING* ON PAGE 71

Hints and tips

How light-hearted or serious the competition is seen to be is up to you. It is worth pointing out the benefits and learning that will come from participating.

Computer-based training (CBT)

At its most basic, CBT is the help screens of most software packages. Moving up the scale, many software packages have a tutorial that is usually an excellent introduction to the software. But CBT is not only about information technology; there are more sophisticated packages available from specialist suppliers in an extraordinary range of subjects from accountancy training to mechanical skills to languages. There are many companies that will design packages to your exact specifications.

For	Against
■ not particularly expensive	■ many people find learning from
■ readily available	the screen more difficult than
■ one-off payment for the	the printed page
package that can be used	■ can make assumptions about
by many people	computer literacy and
■ designed by experts	knowledge of computer
■ very specific to the subject	jargon
■ can be used at several	■ often such a mass of
levels, from extremely basic	information that they can
up to advanced	seem daunting
■ everyone gets the same	■ need careful planning to get
level of training	the best from them
■ can often be printed out	■ not necessarily specific to the
for those who prefer to	way that your company may
learn from a manual	use the package
■ allows users to work at	■ not all packages check the
their own pace	learning that has taken place
■ most packages teach	■ user needs to be monitored to
'best practice' rather than	prevent physical strain
short cuts	from sitting at a screen for
■ good for factual	long periods of time
information.	■ most packages tell 'how' but
	not 'why'
	■ often necessary to update
	'bespoke' packages
	regularly – at a price!
	■ not so successful for
	behavioural skills, which need
	personal feedback.

Finding help

If the package comes with the software, talk to users who already use it. They may well have hints and tips that will help.

Chartered Institute of Personnel and Development

Customer Satisfaction Survey

We would be grateful if you could spend a few minutes answering these questions and return the postcard to CIPD. <u>Please use a black pen to answer.</u> If you would like to receive a free CIPD pen, please include your name and address. IPD MEMBER Y/N

....

1. Title of book ....

2. Date of purchase: month .... year ....

3. How did you acquire this book?
☐ Bookshop ☐ Mail order ☐ Exhibition ☐ Gift ☐ Bought from Author

4. If ordered by mail, how long did it take to arrive:
☐ 1 week ☐ 2 weeks ☐ more than 2 weeks

5. Name of shop .... Town....................................... Country ....

6. Please grade the following according to their influence on your purchasing decision with 1 as least influential: (please tick)

	1	2	3	4	5
Title					
Publisher					
Author					
Price					
Subject					
Cover					

7. On a scale of 1 to 5 (with 1 as poor & 5 as excellent) please give your impressions of the book in terms of: (please tick)

	1	2	3	4	5
Cover design					
Paper/print quality					
Good value for money					
General level of service					

8. Did you find the book:
Covers the subject in sufficient depth ☐ Yes ☐ No
Useful for your work ☐ Yes ☐ No

9. Are you using this book to help:
☐ In your work ☐ Personal study ☐ Both ☐ Other (please state)

Please complete if you are using this as part of a course

10. Name of academic institution...

11. Name of course you are following? ....

12. Did you find this book relevant to the syllabus? ☐ Yes ☐ No ☐ Don't know

Thank you!
To receive regular information about CIPD books and resources call 020 8263 3387.

Any data or information provided to the CIPD for the purposes of membership and other Institute activities will be processed by means of a computer database or otherwise. You may, from time to time, receive business information relevant to your work from the Institute and its other activities. If you do not wish to receive such information please write to the CIPD, giving your full name, address and postcode. The Institute does not make its membership lists available to any outside organisation.

1795/05/00

BUSINESS REPLY SERVICE
Licence No WD 1019

Publishing Department

Chartered Institute of Personnel and Development

CIPD House

Camp Road

Wimbledon

London

SW19 4BR

If you are looking for a supplier for a 'bespoke' CBT package, ask for a reference site and look at other packages that they have produced. CBT producers often have the technical expertise needed but may not be so good at designing the learning component.

These are the things that you need to look out for:

■ What is the basic starting level – will the developee need any other knowledge before using the package?
■ Is it up to date (the latest version)?
■ Is it interesting to use? Some packages are so boring that the developee becomes demotivated and will find excuses to avoid using them.

Setting it up

■ Set clear goals for each session or set of sessions (eg can you learn how to input data and format it this week, and then next week look at how to retrieve that data according to different criteria?).
■ Find a quiet room where the user can work uninterrupted.
■ Make sure that the user knows that a specific time has been set aside for learning and that this will not be interrupted.
■ Set specific tasks that need to be done that are similar to real tasks that will occur in the workplace.
■ Try not to cancel the learning sessions because other work takes priority. This can be hard, but when people are learning incrementally (building their skills up from day to day), a gap in the sessions leads to forgetfulness and sets them back quite significantly.
■ Remember to check that the learning sessions are actually taking place and find out regularly how they feel about things – it is a lonely business sitting hunched over a computer with no chance to get or give feedback.

Resources and people needed

- a quiet working room
- hardware
- software
- any associated manuals, notebooks and paper.

Checking on learning

- Can the developee do the task? (Do not expect perfection too quickly!)
- Has the developee started to feel comfortable with the task?
- Has the developee found a way (if this is possible) to do the task more efficiently?
- Could the developee demonstrate the new skills if asked to?

Similar activities

The most readily available material is in the 'Help' function that is available with almost every software package.

Hints and tips

- Encourage learners to repeat and practise each new skill as they go along – it is necessary to reinforce new skills to make them stick.
- If using a bespoke package, working in a group is very effective – this leads to discussion, clarification and group feedback – all essential parts of the learning cycle.
- The very first session should cover the absolute basics (how to switch on, call up the program, print out, close down etc). If the learner is not comfortable with these, the actual tasks included in the package will seem more daunting than they actually are.

Delegation

This is one of the most useful and used methods for developing your people. Delegation is basically the passing over of a job from one person to another, along with the kudos, praise and reward for doing the job. Delegation takes time, planning and effort; it is *not* just a way of getting rid of all of those nasty tasks that you hate performing!

For	Against
■ gradually develops the skills of the rest of the team	■ many people hate to delegate – they see it as a loss of control
■ the delegatee develops at a sensible pace	■ careless delegation leads to careless performance
■ good delegation keeps a watchful eye on the job until it is obvious that the delegatee is competent.	■ the wrong jobs are often delegated.

Finding help
Who to delegate to

■ people who will be doing the job in the future
■ people who will be standing in for you when you are not there
■ people who need experience in the job area concerned.

Who not to delegate to

■ people who have neither the skill nor the need nor the inclination to do the job
■ people who already have an overcrowded schedule
■ people who would feel demotivated or demeaned by doing the job (either because they are at too high a level to do it, or who would feel that you are simply passing on 'scut work' to them).

What to delegate

- everyday tasks that are important to the business but do not require your high level of expertise
- tasks that will significantly increase the business skills of the people who will be doing them in future
- your absolutely favourite tasks that you know you spend far too long on
- tasks where – although the definition of the task and its quality can be decided by you – you may not have the knowledge or skill to do them yourself
- tasks that you know can be better performed by a specific member of your team.

What not to delegate

- praise and feedback to your team
- disciplinary action
- strategic planning at your management level
- motivational activities.

Setting it up

- You must plan the delegation timetable.
- You must get agreement with the delegatee that he or she is willing to do the task.
- You must be prepared to spend considerable time making sure that the delegation process is fully covered.

Resources and people needed

Time is the main resource needed. One of the main reasons that people do not delegate properly is that they think 'I could do it myself in half the time it would take me to delegate it.' This is true, but it does mean that you will never be able to hand the task on! So grit your teeth and think of all the time you will save later on.

The delegation process

Delegation stage	What to do
1 Examine the tasks that you are about to delegate.	Define the tasks – exactly what is involved in the task, what are the results, what are the quality standards, what are the timescales, why is the task important to the group?
2 Talk through the implications of the task with the delegatee.	Make absolutely sure that the delegatee understands what will be expected of him or her and just what the completed task will look like.
3 Demonstrate the task to the delegatee.	Do this slowly, explaining each stage as you go along and encouraging the delegatee to ask questions and ask you to repeat anything that isn't fully understood. Do not hurry this stage.
4 Ask the delegate to do the task, explaining him/herself as he or she goes along. Watch as he or she is performing it.	Watch carefully. Are all the stages being covered? If the delegatee makes a mistake (and they often will!), don't jump down their throat; stop them gently and ask what is happening. You have to walk a fine line between keeping quality standards high and allowing the natural experimentation that is a part of learning.
5 Discuss how they thought they did and how you thought they did.	Remember the rules of feedback – start with a positive then move on to the areas that need more attention.
6 Ask them to do the task, but this time don't watch them.	Make sure that they know that you are available should they need you, but don't stand over them. Encourage them to ask for help should they need you.
7 After they have done the task on their own for the second time, discuss how they thought they did and how you thought they did.	Remember the rules of feedback. Ask them if they could think of a better way to do the task that would lead to just as high quality a result. Encourage them to find their own way of working without compromising the outcomes.
8 Hand the task over to them and retire gracefully.	They are now in charge of the task; all they have to do is report back to you when they have finished.
9 Delegation is complete.	Feed back their success to them.

Checking on learning

Just because you have delegated the task does not mean that you have delegated the responsibility of keeping the group up to standards. Particularly in the first month or so after successfully delegating, check up that standards are still high; remember to give feedback and praise where necessary.

Hints and tips

Patience, patience, patience! When you are showing people how to do something that you are thoroughly familiar with you will probably go far too fast and confuse them, so *slow down*; care taken at this point will save hours later.

Demonstration

This is where you can capitalise on the expertise within your team and company. It is particularly useful when introducing new technology or practices. Unless it is imperative that everyone must be up to speed with the new skill all at once, an effectively designed set of demonstrations allows you to dedicate just *one* person's time to the in-depth learning process. They can then pass the information on to larger groups in a time-effective manner. There is also no reason why the suppliers of the new technology should not provide working demonstrations to you and your team as part of the sales process (see pages 49–52).

For	Against
■ cost-effective	■ the demonstration needs to be tailored to real life and should not cover aspects that are unlikely to be used
■ effective demonstrations cover the information and processes used in your own team or company	
■ time-effective.	■ the demonstrator needs time to prepare.

Finding help

Sales support, product management teams, and research and development departments are mines of information and skill.

They are also used to demonstrating to customers. Do not over-look some of the sources nearer to hand – I once worked in a large company who successfully introduced word processing to the entire company by using its secretarial staff as demonstra-tors. Its reasoning was that these were the people who worked every day with the package and so knew exactly how it was and should be used in the company.

Setting it up

- As usual, find out exactly how people are going to be using the new technology or practice in the real world.
- Select your demonstrator and give him or her time to learn the new technology or practice.
- Train the demonstrator.
- Schedule and run the demonstration sessions.

Training the demonstrator
First the demonstrator needs to be thoroughly familiar with his or her subject – not only what to do but also what to do if things go wrong. This is not a selling demo where everything is perfect, but a working demo where the user is the focus – not the tech-nology or the process. It is useful if the demonstrator keeps a note of the things that they found complex or difficult to learn and where they found it difficult to understand exactly why something should be done in a particular way. These points can then be highlighted during the demo.

The demonstrator then needs to look through any user manuals and highlight the really important sections.

A really successful teaching demonstration needs an agenda. Here is an example:

- **logistics** – timing, who is who, what help is available, need to take notes etc

- **overview** – what the technology or process does and how it will be useful
- **basic information** – starting up, closing down, safety issues etc
- **distribution and introduction** – of any user manuals, documentation or checklists that might be useful
- **introduction of first module** – what will be covered, points to watch out for, how and why these procedures are needed
- **demonstration of first module** – follow the sequence: 'Tell. Show. Explain. Show again. Take questions. Check learning. Link to the next module.'

To illustrate this sequence, let's take an example. Suppose you were demonstrating how to use a video camera. One of the first modules might go like this:

- **Tell** – 'This part of the demo will cover how to cable up from the mains, switch on, insert the tape and start recording. Here are the things you will need.'
- **Show** – 'This is the camera, the mains power cable and the tape. The power cable fits into the camera here and plugs into this socket on the wall. Switch the power on at the wall and then switch the camera on using the ribbed POWER switch located here. You will see the little red power light here come on. You can now open the tape cassette holder by pressing the EJECT button and insert the tape, label side out, like this... close the cassette holder by pressing its centre area like this. You now press the REC standby button and the camera is ready to record when you press the red START/STOP button here...'
- **Explain** – 'Nothing on the camera will function until the power is switched on, both at the wall and on the camera itself.'
- **Show again** – 'So to recap, mains power in here at the wall and here at the camera. Camera power on here, REC standby

mode is switched on here and to start recording you press START/STOP here.'

- **Take questions** – 'Are there any questions – any worries about the difference between standby mode and actually starting to record?'
- **Check learning** – 'Would one of you like to try?'
- **Link to next module** – 'Now that we know how to start up, we need to check that the camera is in focus and how to zoom in and out. As before, until the camera is powered on, none of the functions will work.'

Now this may all seem very long-winded and slow, but that is the secret of a good training demonstration. Leave nothing to chance, repeat yourself often, make no assumptions about base knowledge level and always check that learning has taken place.

Questions the demonstrator needs to ask before giving a demonstration

- Who will be there?
- What is their job?
- How are they going to use the new information?
- What is their skill level?
- How much do they already know?
- What do they want to see? (each and every one of them?)
- What are you trying to achieve in this demo?
- How long will you need?
- How will you pace the demonstration to make it fascinating?
- What questions do you expect?
- What do you want them to do after the demonstration?

Resources and people needed

- demonstration equipment (including any charts, projectors etc)

- scheduled time for the sessions
- space (unless the groups are very small).

Checking on learning

Get them to demonstrate back to you!

Similar activities

> SEE *COACHING* ON PAGE 42; *FIND THE EXPERT* ON PAGE 64;
> *SHADOWING* ON PAGE 89; *SIT BY NELLIE* ON PAGE 91; *SUPPLIER
> TRAINING* ON PAGE 93

Hints and tips

- Allow enough time for the demonstrator to prepare.
- Do not hurry the demonstration – take time.
- Always check for learning.
- Ensure that the audience has the chance to try for themselves while their memories of the demonstration are fresh.
- Have a helpline of some sort for new learners.

Feedback

This is the most effective way of developing your people. Feedback is vital if they are to improve. Lack of feedback is probably the most demotivating feature of any job. Feedback itself is simply telling employees how they, their group and the company is performing, what they are doing well, what they need to improve and what changes need to be made. Even when everything is going well, there is still the need to feed that back to them. Feedback should be encouraged throughout the group – not just from the manager to the employee, but across the function and from the bottom up.

For	Against
■ gives an instant result	■ if the feedback sessions are well
■ strengthens bonds between the group and the manager	run – nothing!
■ allows both sides to look at specific, real problems	
■ highly motivating	
■ no cost	
■ part of the necessary quality control function of the manager	
■ leads to quick development of employees.	

Finding help

Anyone in your group can give feedback – the only rule is that the feedback must have a specific purpose and should lead to either increased motivation or the correction of unsatisfactory performance. For this reason, any feedback session should happen in an atmosphere of openness, there must be no hidden agendas and it should *never* be used to score points or belittle.

Resources and people needed

■ uninterrupted time
■ privacy if some of the feedback might be perceived as negative
■ time for all of the people involved to join in
■ something to keep notes in.

Checking on learning

Use the next feedback session to see how things are shaping up.

Similar activities

■ quality meetings
■ progress meetings
■ job assessment interviews.

Feedback rules

Feedback rule	How to make it happen
1 Start with a positive.	Open the feedback session by concentrating on what has been done well and exactly why those particular actions or behaviours were successful.
2 Encourage the person receiving the feedback to join in and contribute as soon as possible.	Feedback must be a two-way process if it is to be useful. Getting people to talk about what they have done causes them to examine their actions far more effectively than just thinking about them.
3 When giving feedback that is trying to correct mistakes or poor working practices, ask the developee what *they* would like to change before you jump in with your comments.	There is always a tendency to start off by praising what has been done well and then bring the dreaded 'but . . .' (which sadly makes everything you've said before the 'but' sound like a lie!). If you ask for their comments about what needs to be changed before you put in your twopence-worth, you can can avoid this. You may also be pleasantly surprised at the insight that most of us show about our shortcomings!
4 Feedback must concentrate on behaviours and results.	Knowing how someone feels about what is going on is all very well – but it won't necessarily bring about any changes. Concentrating on what has actually happened and discussing what can be changed to make things better is much more positive.
5 Focus on observations rather than opinions.	You can only feed back truthfully on what you yourself have observed. Working on hearsay or other people's opinions is a minefield. This is not to say that the opinions of others are not valid, just that you need to be able to cite actual examples if your feedback is to be believed.

6 Focus on descriptions rather than judgements.	For example, 'We seem to be spending a long time copy-editing the proposals we are putting out – can we have a go at using the spell checker more rigorously?', is a better approach than, 'You illiterate ***!XX*** – use the spell checker!'
7 Be specific, not general.	Just as praise should be specific, so should correction or criticism. Unless the specific problem is highlighted, there will never be a specific fix.
8 Share ideas, don't give advice.	If the developee is not involved in the proposed solution, you are wasting your (and their) time. You can offer help and support, but in the end it is the developee who is going to change – not you.
9 Be sensitive to how the feedback is received.	Some people accept feedback more easily than others. There is no golden rule that says we should accept everything we are told. People become very sensitive when mistakes or negative behaviours are pointed out and become very defensive, which will slow the feedback session down. Allow for this; you are trying for a win/win situation where the focus is on solving the problem, not on casting or excusing blame.
10 End the feedback session by planning future actions (on both sides).	After any feedback session there should be an active outcome – 'Keep up the good work' or 'Let's try it this way . . .' Try to end up with a realistic list of actions.

Hints and tips

■ Make a firm date for the next session.
■ Encourage an atmosphere of openness in the group so that people are not worried about admitting that things are not

going as well as possible. The more open you are with the group, the more open they will be with you.

■ Encourage an atmosphere of best practice in the group; you can do this by having regular meetings where better ways of working are discussed without citing particular individuals or behaviours.

Find the expert

Do you have a database of all the courses that the people on your team have attended? Do you have a list of the skill sets of each of your team members? Do you have a list of the people you go to in order to solve problems or find out up-to-date information? If you do, you have a ready-made pool of expertise to help your people develop their skills and knowledge base. Do you have a company library? A cuttings file of articles and papers written by industry and business leaders? Videos of presentations given by recognised industry leaders? All of these form the expertise that you can make available to your team.

For	Against
■ once set up, fairly cheap to run ■ you get high-quality input from the experts.	■ you need someone to keep the database/library up to date – in terms of both availability and contact numbers on the part of the people on it and the relevance of the material contained in it; this can be time-consuming.

Finding help

Keep your eyes and ears open – never let an expert pass by if you can help it. When you run company courses or conferences, record the expert speakers on tape or video if possible. Have a judicious mix of reading matter and live bodies that you can use.

Setting it up

■ Dedicate an efficient space to your list of experts and expert advice (not some desolate filing cabinet that no one knows about).
■ Appoint someone to keep it up to date.
■ Let everyone in your team know that this pool of expertise exists and how to use it.

Resources and people needed

■ space and time
■ a good filing system
■ a 'librarian'.

Similar activities

SEE *MENTORING* ON PAGE 82; *SHADOWING* ON PAGE 89

Hints and tips

Do not let any particular expert become overburdened with requests for help – they have their own work to do as well.

Formal training courses

Practically all managers will be aware of the value of formal training courses, and indeed, training courses are a pretty painless way of developing your people in terms of personal effort (if not quite so painless in budget terms). I define formal training as: courses delivered by professional trainers. You may have access to a training department within your company. If not, there are literally hundreds, if not thousands, of training companies and training consultants available to you. (See also 'Public and private bodies' on page 83.) I do not intend to give more than general guidelines here and refer you to the CIPD's Training Essentials series for more in-depth information (www.cipd.co.uk/publications/).

For	Against
■ professional trainers	■ cost
■ 'even playing field' approach where all staff get the same level of training for company-wide courses	■ if 'bespoke' and run only for your company, you need to fill the course and this may mean having an entire team away from their desks all at once
■ 'open' courses (where the audience is made up of a range of companies) allow you to send individuals on courses	■ external trainers may not be familiar with your company, markets or products.
■ can be tailored to your needs.	

Finding help

Many training companies are accredited by public bodies or manufacturers; this usually means that they know what they are doing. Accreditation is not so usual with companies or consultants dealing in the softer, behavioural skills needed in business. If you have not had a recommendation (one of the best ways of judging the quality of a training company), you will need to find out as much as you can about them before you let them loose on your people. Contact one of their existing clients and see what they think. Certainly interview the trainer and ask to see an itemised course agenda and course details. Here is a checklist of the sort of questions you should be asking:

■ What experience have they had in the field you are asking them to train in? Ask for reference sites.

■ What pre-course preparation is needed by the participants? A good trainer will help you with the necessary briefing that you give to the participants.

■ What documentation is available? Look at the quality – is it pleasant to look at, designed for easy use?

■ What feedback will the trainer give to the participants and to yourself? What sort of course evaluation forms do they supply? If you have existing evaluation forms, are they suitable for this particular course? Will the trainer hold a debrief meeting?

■ What follow-up will the course need? Will the trainer be available to do 'catch-up' training if necessary?

■ What does the trainer know about your markets, products, company and procedures? Will you need to thoroughly brief the trainer? What information can you give them to take away?

■ Can the trainer tailor the course to your exact needs? What will this cost?

■ How much of the organisational burden can the trainer or company take? The less you have to do the better.

■ Who is responsible for paying for the venue (if you are holding the course externally)?

Hints and tips

■ Really careful expectation and objective-setting is vital with formal courses. More courses are damaged by poor expectations and lack of knowledge of the reasons for attending the course *than by any other single factor.*

■ If the course is mandatory, avoid any suggestion (implied or spoken) that the attendee is a failure and must attend the course to improve. Introducing the course as 'another tool for your business skills toolbox' is a far more effective approach than 'attend or else!'

■ Update your 'Experts File' after each course (see page 64).

Group learning

This is where a group of people needing a particular set of skills gets together and, after devising a strategy for learning them, work together to make the learning happen.

For	Against
■ increases the skills of a working group all at once ■ no great expense ■ also acts as a team-building exercise ■ group members motivate each other ■ the group internally tests itself on the new skills or knowledge ■ uses the existing skills of the group.	■ sometimes difficult to arrange a suitable time for all of the group members to be together.

Finding help

The group will need a leader. Choose someone who has one or more of the following attributes:

■ in-depth knowledge of the skill to be learned
■ experience of the tasks to be learned
■ enthusiasm for the idea of learning as a group
■ good communication skills (not only their ability to communicate, but the skill to encourage others to communicate)
■ good networking skills.

The leader will kick off the group learning sessions and make sure that everyone knows when and where the meetings are. The first meeting is spent plotting the methodologies that the group might use. They might choose discussion, role plays, demonstrations and so on.

Setting it up

■ Set the objectives carefully and work out how you will measure the success of the learning project (for example, if the objectives were: 'to learn, as a group, the use, features and benefits of product A', then the success might be measured by a group presentation and demonstration).

■ Carefully brief the leader on the learning project – why it is necessary, what resources are available, who will be in the group and how success will be measured.

■ Make sure that time and space are set aside for the group to achieve the objectives.

■ Set a reasonable timescale (open-ended timescales do not lead to any sense of urgency).

■ Debrief with the group after they have completed the task(s) and make a note of what worked well and what could be done better next time.

Resources and people needed

■ enough time set aside for the learning project!

Checking on learning

If you have set the objectives carefully, you will have decided what the measures will be.

Hints and tips

■ If you are using group learning regularly, make sure that you rotate the leadership around the group.

■ Reward the whole group for their effort and success with a group outing, party or get-together.

Immersion

Here, developees are completely on their own – no trainers, no mentors, no advice, no help, no immediate feedback. They find out what they need to know or do it simply by trial and error. It sounds terrible but all of us have done it at some time or another; in fact, some people actually like to learn in this way. They go along at their own pace, with no preconceptions to distract them. Although I do not recommend this method for very inexperienced team members, it can be very effective for skilled people who have good basic skills but still need to develop them further.

For	Against
■ people can work at their own pace	■ it is lonely
■ people learn in a real situation	■ it can be demotivating working on your own without feedback
■ no cost in money terms.	■ no correction of bad habits
	■ longer learning curve.

Setting it up

■ There is not a great deal that needs to be done. That said, however, it saves time and frustration for the developee if the infrastructures underlying the tasks to be learned are as efficient as possible. For example, the developee should know where all the necessary tools and resources are kept.

■ Suggest that some sort of record might be kept. This is not for your use, but as a tool to help the developee to keep track of what he or she has learned – there will be so much going on that it is useful to encourage the developee to sit down at the end of each day and consolidate his or her learning.

Resources and people needed

■ an orderly working area and all the necessary tools.

Checking on learning

Encourage the developee to report to you at regular intervals.

Hints and tips

■ Feedback, recognition that you are doing the job more effectively, attention and support are great motivators; be sure that the developee knows that you have noticed and value the new skills that are developing.

■ Make sure that the developee has opportunities to practise and refine the new skills.

Induction training

This is the process, formal or informal, that introduces newcomers to your company or your group. Ideally it should take place as soon as possible after the new member has arrived. Formal induction courses are typically run company-wide and concentrate on a general introduction to the company and its structure, people, working practices, processes, products, clients and suppliers. For large companies this is a very necessary procedure if the newcomers are to take advantage of the resources supplied by the company. Smaller companies may not need a formal induction course, but efforts must be made to familiarise the newcomer as quickly as possible. Changing jobs or starting with a new group is a stressful time for anyone and a good induction process takes a great deal of this stress away.

For	Against
■ gets the newcomer up to speed quickly	■ may require considerable time and effort from other members of staff
■ gives a unified set of messages about the company	■ can be expensive in terms of time and labour
■ very motivating – the newcomer feels welcomed and supported	■ formal induction courses are usually run only once a year, which is very often far too late for some of the newcomers.
■ gives the people involved a chance to assess what the company is really supposed to be doing.	

Finding help

Usually, formal induction courses are organised by the human resources department, which also makes sure that the employees' terms and conditions are explained to them. If the HR department is not involved, then each group would organise its own process.

Setting it up

■ Make a list of all the things that the newcomer needs to know. Typically these fall into three main areas, as illustrated in the table below.

Infrastructure, business tasks and products and services

Infrastructure	Business tasks	Products and services
✓ the geography of the building/s	✓ job descriptions and responsibilities	✓ the products and services your company supplies
✓ where everything is	✓ budgets and targets	
✓ how to use basic tools (telephones, e-mail, intranet, messaging etc)	✓ quality standards	✓ the markets your company is involved with
	✓ how the new group member will be assessed and evaluated	✓ your company's customers
✓ who does what, organisation charts		
✓ procedures (expenses, overtime, health and safety, confidentiality, purchasing, invoicing etc)	✓ where to find expert advice and help	✓ your company's suppliers
		✓ terms of business (where applicable)
		✓ future plans (where applicable)
✓ company history		

■ Set aside a specific time when the newcomer can meet all the people in your department.
■ Make certain that the first day that the newcomer joins your group is carefully planned and meet him or her personally on arrival.

- The newcomer's working space and associated tools and equipment should be ready for them, as should any necessary badges, passes, keys and so on.
- Do not expect immediate productivity – although it is useful if you map out some of the essential tasks that the newcomer will be tackling day to day.
- Appoint an experienced member of your team as a 'guide' who can act as adviser and support during the first few weeks.

Resources and people needed

- company literature
- terms and conditions of employment
- health and safety information, procedures, manuals and literature.

Checking on learning

Keep a close eye on the inductee and make sure that you are available to them during the first few weeks. There is no need to featherbed new team members, but it is vital that they feel that you are keeping a weather eye out for them. Even experienced and confident individuals feel unsure when in a new situation, and keeping their comfort levels high is an essential management task at this point. Indeed, the relationship that is made in these early days sets the pattern for the months to come.

Hints and tips

- Think back to when you were new to the company – what were the things that you needed to know?
- Don't schedule a heavy workload for the first week.
- Put aside a half hour each day for a meeting with the newcomer so that you can check how they are getting on and whether they have any worries.

Internet/e-learning

There are hundreds of e-learning sites on the World Wide Web. Both interactive and screen-based programmes are available. It is important to encourage your team to use the Internet as a source of 'just-in-time' information and training. It is useful to check that perfectly sensible company policies against misuse of the Internet do not frighten your team so much that they regard all Internet use as forbidden.

For	Against
■ readily available	■ sometimes very general and
■ not particularly expensive	needs to be backed up with
■ very often written by experts	more company-specific material
who really know what	■ there is so much material
they are doing	available that it takes a while
■ the developee can work	to assess the usefulness and
at his or her own pace.	quality of the material.

This is such an enormous subject and growing so rapidly that it needs a book to itself. For more information about the value of e-learning, see *The E-Learning Revolution: From propositions to action* by Martyn Sloman (CIPD, 2001).

Intranet

This refers to a company-wide knowledge base available through the developee's computer. It works in the same way as any website but has the advantage that the information contained in it is specific to your company's products, services, procedures and customers. It is an excellent source of information for a newcomer to the company and is often used as part of the induction process (see page 71).

Job swapping

This is where you take someone's job over for a specified time (not the 'Fill in for her until she comes back from holiday' scenario, but 'Go and find out what doing her job entails and how it interacts with yours').

This is a really effective way of sharpening and honing existing skills and avoiding staleness. One of the most effective job swap exercises I have ever seen involved a careless salesman and a diligent order processor. The salesman was used to putting in rather sloppy orders, with the result that the delivered order either had parts missing (underspecification) or wrong components (not reading the specification form carefully) or utterly wrong pricing (overselling). The order processor could not see why the salesman was so apparently careless and the salesman thought that the order processor was being picky. After three days in each other's jobs they had a completely new outlook on how to work together and harmony reigned (for a time at least).

For	Against
■ teaches people how their job is affected by others and gives them an insight into co-operative working	■ not suitable for people on deadlines
■ not expensive	■ must be set up carefully with a good briefing beforehand.
■ sharpens up existing skills	
■ creates useful networks.	

Finding help
Each participant must have the time and the skill to brief each other carefully – it is pointless for the blind to lead the blind.

Setting it up

■ Do not job swap people who have absolutely no idea of what the job they are going to swap to entails and why they would benefit from the exercise.
■ Brief each person carefully on timescales (not more than a few days) and responsibilities.
■ Decide how much initial inefficiency you can put up with (they are not going to be expert in the new job immediately) and make sure that help is at hand.

- Have a briefing day where each explains what they do to the other.
- Swap the jobs.
- Arrange time for them at the end of each day to get together and share what they have learned.
- Negotiate with the respective managers (if necessary) how any skill shortfalls are to be managed.
- Have a debrief session at the end of the job swap.

Resources and people needed

- the swappers
- understanding from the respective managers.

Checking on learning

The final debrief should give you a clear idea of what new skills or understanding are now in place.

Similar activities

SEE *LEARNING BY WALKING ABOUT* ON PAGE 76; *SHADOWING* ON PAGE 89; *SIT BY NELLIE* ON PAGE 91

Hints and tips

- Initially this exercise might seem risky. What if the job swappers mess up the department out of ignorance? In fact this rarely happens. The managers in charge of each department need to keep a serious eye on the job swappers; not necessarily to chastise them – more to offer a helping hand.
- Keep the swappers up to date with any changes that would affect their 'real job'; they should not feel isolated from happenings while they are on the exercise.

Learning by walking about

This is not only a particularly interesting way of helping new employees to understand the company and how the different departments link up but is very useful indeed for all management trainees or indeed anyone moving up the management ladder – even those right at the very top. It is common practice for new managing directors and CEOs to spend several weeks learning by walking about, by which they not only get to know what they are taking on, but also get their faces known.

For	Against
■ little cost	■ might be disruptive if overdone.
■ creates good networks	
■ brings different groups together.	

Finding help

All departments can be involved, but check that they are willing to have visitors and are not working towards vital deadlines.

Setting it up

■ Decide what it is the developee needs to find out and structure the 'walkabout time' logically. Here is an example:

Developee: Sales trainee XXXX

Need: To understand the order fulfilment process and what might impede it

Departments to be visited: XXXX

People to contact: XXXX

End result: Prepare a flow chart showing the step-by-step activities that need to be undertaken from the point where a salesperson takes an order from a customer up to the delivery, post-delivery activities and final payment by the customer.

Highlight any areas where there might be a hold-up because of lack of information from the salesperson.

Resources and people needed

■ planning time (although this make take up time at first, the same exercise can be used over and over again).

Checking on learning
Inspect the final result.

Similar activities

SEE *COMPANY ROADSHOWS* ON PAGE 45; *SHADOWING* ON PAGE 89;
SIT BY NELLIE ON PAGE 91

Hints and tips

- Choose activities to be investigated that have a direct bearing on what the developee does in his or her job.
- Alert the departments to be involved before the exercise starts.

Manuals and reference books

This is learning from the printed page – an age-old methodology! It is one that we have all (or almost all) come across in our life. It is suitable as a back-up for almost all skills (though not totally effective for physical skills where only practice can make perfect).

For	Against
■ easily available	■ usually no practical exercises
■ relatively cheap	■ can be overgeneral – not
■ usually written by experts	tailored particularly to your
■ portable – can be used	needs
anywhere, anytime	■ unless clear goals are set, can
■ non-linear – books and	become a purely intellectual
manuals can be returned	exercise, which may lead to
to again and again.	greater understanding but not
	necessarily greater skills
	■ company libraries are
	time-consuming to run and
	control.

Finding help
Look at book reviews, surf the Web, ask colleagues, look in professional publications, local libraries and national libraries.

Setting it up

- Get the developee to define exactly what they need to learn and how it will be applied.
- Have a clear learning plan with timescales and goals.
- If at all possible, use more than one source.
- If more than one person is learning the same stuff, get them to organise regular meetings where they can discuss what they have discovered.
- Arrange for the developee to present what they have learned to the rest of their group at regular intervals.
- Give them the checklist on pages 80–81 before they begin.

Resources and people needed

- the reference material
- sticky notes, pens and pencils
- a quiet space
- uninterrupted time
- perseverance!

Checking on learning

- Can the developee do the task? (Do not expect perfection too quickly!)
- Can the developee explain to others what they have learned?
- Has the developee found a way (if this is possible) to do the task more efficiently?

Hints and tips

- Check when the books/manuals were published. Outdated information is worse than useless.
- Since reading is a solitary pastime, make sure that the developee is not left out of group activities.

Learning from the printed page

This is an efficient way to go about learning things from the written page. It gets things into the memory easily and helps you to retain the facts longer. It may look cumbersome at first, but it's well worth the effort.

Learning stage	What to do
1 Lay the foundations	❑ Look through the written material.
	❑ Have a notebook, pack of sticky notes and coloured pens handy.
	❑ Make yourself familiar with what each book or manual contains and where it is in the book, read the cover blurb, look at the contents page and the index.
	❑ Flip through the books/manuals and find out where the footnotes and references are.
	❑ If you come across anything that really interests you, write the subject down on a sticky note and stick it into the relevant page.
	❑ If there are any summary paragraphs or sections, read through these.
	❑ Do *not* start to systematically read the whole book/manual yet.
2 Encourage active reading	❑ Write down a set of questions to which you need the answers.
	❑ These questions should relate to your day-to-day work.
	❑ Think in chunks – for example, if you were trying to learn how to mend a television, think about the different groups of tasks that you would need to master (identifying the different parts of the TV, finding the tools necessary, knowing the common faults and their symptoms etc . . .).
	❑ Keep these questions by you as you read, and when you find the answers either tick them off or write them down.
	❑ As new questions occur to you, write them down.
	❑ Refer to the questions before each study session.

3 **Study the text and diagrams**	❑ Read the text. ❑ Don't try to read everything. Set yourself a number of questions to answer and concentrate on those. ❑ When you come across things that you don't fully understand, re-scan the text and try to guess what the answer might be. ❑ Mark any questions that you still cannot answer – you can find the answers later. ❑ Relate everything you read to the real world. ❑ Don't read for too long – 20 minutes is quite enough without a break.
4 **Verbalise what you have learned**	❑ Talk to yourself while you are reading. ❑ Answer your questions out loud. ❑ Talk to your colleagues and ask for their input. ❑ Until you can explain something aloud you have not fully learned it.
5 **Test your learning**	❑ Set yourself little quizzes and tests. Devise exercises that you can use in the real world to see if you fully understand what you are supposed to do. (To go back to the television example, look at a real television and name the parts, look at the tools and describe what each one is for, when you see a fault, try to guess what may have caused it . . .) **Do this without the book/manual.**
6 **Unify what you have learned**	❑ Think about how your new knowledge fits with what you already knew. ❑ If you had preconceptions that you now know to be false, try hard to get rid of them.
7 **Practise your new knowledge**	❑ Use your new information in the real world as fast as possible; test the boundaries. ❑ Go through your entire list of questions and see if you can still remember the answers. ❑ Refine your skills – see if you can find better ways of doing things. Most books and manuals don't teach short cuts – you need to find these out for yourself.

Mentoring

This is one of the oldest and most successful methods for developing individuals within your team. The mentoring process has been going on throughout history.

A mentor is a trusted counsellor and guide – usually someone who not only has an effective set of relevant skills but who also has a breadth of experience in business practices, company processes and the problems facing someone in a new job or situation. This could be someone within your group, or indeed anyone within the company. Like puppies – a mentor is not just for Christmas but often for a lifetime.

For	Against
■ gives the developee a central reference point for problems and difficulties	■ busy mentors may often find it hard to make time for their 'mentees'.
■ a good mentor can interpret the company's needs and standards from a real-life viewpoint	
■ no cost.	

Finding help

Mentors must be prepared to meet regularly with their mentees. They act as role models, interpreters of company attitudes and behaviours, advisers and guides. A good mentoring relationship is based on mutual trust and respect. Quite often the developee will choose their own mentor, although this may be difficult for newcomers to the company. As a manager you will certainly know people in your management group who would make good mentors.

There is a golden rule about mentoring: 'Never interrupt or abuse the mentoring process.' This means that what goes on between the mentor and mentee is private and not disclosed. You should not ask the mentor how things are going and you should not interrogate the mentee about the effectiveness of the mentor. To do so would threaten the entire process.

There is a very useful book to help with the mentoring process: *Everyone Needs a Mentor: Fostering talent at work* (3rd edn) by David Clutterbuck (CIPD, 2001).

Setting it up

- You act as a 'marriage broker' between the developee and the person acting as mentor.
- Make sure that the mentee knows that the relationship they have with their mentor is not one of manager and subordinate, more that of a trusted friend and guide.
- You do not relinquish your duties as a manager.

Resources and people needed

- a pool of people who could and would act as a mentor – nothing more!

Similar activities

- apprenticeships.

Hints and tips

Generous thanks are due to anyone who takes on the role of mentor. Touch base often with the people who are mentoring your group and make sure that they know how much they are appreciated by you.

Public/private bodies

Practically all professions have a trade or member organisation where they share information and skills. In addition to these are the more generalised professional bodies like the Chartered Institute of Personnel and Development, the Industrial Society, the Institute of Directors, the Law Society, the Chartered Institute of Engineers and so on. Government departments (particularly the Department of Trade and Industry) also offer vast quantities of information on business law and practices. The Open University, Local Education Authorities and National Council for Vocational Qualifications offer a huge range of courses. A quick look through any local directory will give you an idea of just how much resource there is out there. These bodies are an invaluable source for developing your people. For the price of membership you have the availability of magazines, websites, seminars, exhibitions, training, advice and up-to-the minute information – not just about your particular business but about your customers' and clients' businesses too. The opportunities for networking are immense.

For	Against
■ huge range of information available	■ membership fees can be high.
■ expert advice	
■ in-depth knowledge of individual areas of business	
■ professional standards.	

Finding help
A charter denotes excellence. Accreditation ensures that any qualifications gained are of a required and recognised standard.

Setting it up
Join the club and have a look at what is on offer. Subscribe to your trade organisation and read its publications.

Resources and people needed

■ subscription fees and time.

Quality circles

The concept of quality circles came into being in the 1950s. It basically consists of a small group (6–10) of workers and supervisors who are all concerned with a particular set of business processes and work together as a group. They hold regular meetings (once a week). They choose a quality issue, find out why it is happening, come up with a solution and take corrective action. The quality circle takes responsibility for solving the problem.

Management is involved in helping to identify which problems need to be investigated and with the evaluation and final decisions; the rest is up to the quality circle.

The figure below shows the process they go through.

Quality circles

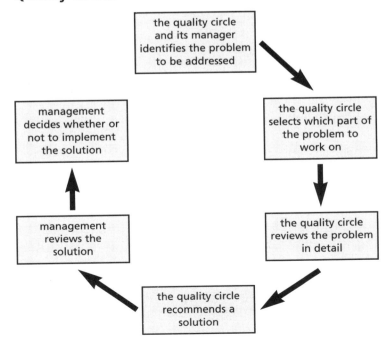

For	Against
■ works with real-life problems	■ if not properly introduced or supported it can easily be seen as a fruitless exercise
■ highly motivational	
■ high level of information-sharing among the group	■ if management consistently ignores the quality circle's recommendations, the group becomes demotivated
■ increases communication, problem-solving and planning skills	
■ leads to higher-quality standards.	■ regular time needs to be dedicated to the exercise – this requires good timetabling.

Setting it up

The group may require initial training in the skills needed to run successful meetings and solve problems. On page 87 you can find the sort of reminder sheet that would help with problem-solving.

Resources and people needed

■ a meeting room
■ dedicated time for the meetings.

Checking on learning

The problem should be solved!

Similar activities

SEE *BEST PRACTICE GROUPS* ON PAGE 35; *CASE STUDIES* ON PAGE 36

Hints and tips

■ Publicly acknowledge the contribution of the quality circle. Publish their findings in company magazines and on the intranet.
■ Encourage the quality circle to find a real sense of identity (they may like to give themselves a name, for example).
■ Encourage the group to put an actual value on their contributions.

Group problem-solving flow chart

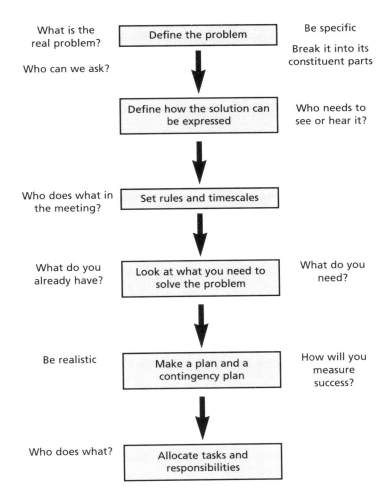

What is the
real problem?

Who can we ask?

Define the problem

Be specific

Break it into its
constituent parts

Define how the solution can
be expressed

Who needs to
see or hear it?

Who does what in
the meeting?

Set rules and timescales

What do you
already have?

Look at what you need to
solve the problem

What do you
need?

Be realistic

Make a plan and a
contingency plan

How will you
measure
success?

Who does what?

Allocate tasks and
responsibilities

Role play

A role play is where two or more people take the parts of protagonists in a business interaction. It is not an acting session, but a way of exploring possible ways of behaving. It is a very useful tool when you find that one of your team is having particular difficulties in a situation that involves interaction with others.

Typical situations might be such things as conflict management, sales skills, management skills and customer handling. It is also very effective when developing skills such as telephone handling, order taking and handling complaints. One of the most effective ways of using role play is when debriefing your team members after an activity that has not gone completely as you would have hoped (things like failed sales calls, poor handling of customers, conflict between team members). If you can 'replay' what happened and try to devise a strategy that would correct the situation while the memories are still strong, then the learning from such a session is immediate and lasting.

For	Against
■ provides a chance to explore alternative behaviours in a non-threatening atmosphere ■ allows people to 'wear the other person's shoes' ■ no expense ■ very specific if set up well.	■ some people absolutely loathe role playing – they find it artificial and possibly risky (in this case – ask them to observe the role play and give feedback on what they see and hear rather than participate in the role play itself) ■ must be carefully set up.

Setting it up

■ Define exactly what needs to be investigated during the role play.

■ Get the developee to describe the situation as clearly and in as much detail as possible. (This, by the way, is the starting point for change; often just the action of clearly describing what has happened is enough to point the way clearly to the solution.)

■ Decide which part each of you will play (you should try to take each part in turn).

■ Start the role play.

■ When problems arrive, take 'time out' and discuss what is going wrong.

- Restart the role play and try again.
- When the role play is finished, debrief carefully and draw up an action plan for the future.

Resources and people needed

- time
- private space.

Checking on learning
This should be apparent from the role play.

Hints and tips

- Do not force role plays on people who see them as play-acting or threatening.
- Ensure that the developee plays both sides of the role play so that they can gain an understanding of what the other person was feeling.

Shadowing

This is where the developee simply follows another more knowledgeable or skilled member of staff about and learns from what they observe of the expert's actions and contacts. It is an extremely effective method of introducing new and inexperienced staff to the various functions within your group or company. It is not as timetabled or organised as learning by walking about (see page 76) or sit by Nellie (see page 91). The only limitation involved is a timescale – after a few hours of shadowing it is important to get the developee to actually do something useful. It is a gentle introduction to working practices and for this reason is very useful for school leavers with no concept of what business is like.

For	Against
■ no cost ■ introduces new members of staff to the company and group very effectively ■ sets clear expectations for working practices.	■ if it goes on too long the developee will get bored, and want to get on with meaningful work ■ not suitable if the shadow has to sit for a long time watching someone thinking rather than carrying out tasks; the whole point of shadowing is that the shadow does not interrupt the person they are shadowing.

Finding help

Pick the person to be shadowed carefully. As I said above, the developee simply watches what is going on, without interrupting or questioning the person they are watching. Naturally they will talk to the person they are shadowing, but it is not necessary that they are rigorously taught anything at this point. If the person they are shadowing has the sort of job that requires a great deal of silent and non-interactive activity, it can become tedious and demotivating for the shadow.

Setting it up

- Work out what you want the shadow to observe. Try to pick the sort of tasks and skills that are interesting and useful to watch.
- Introduce the shadow to the group and let them get on with it.
- Have a debrief session where you find out what the shadow has learned.

Similar activities

SEE *LEARNING BY WALKING ABOUT* ON PAGE 76; *SIT BY NELLIE* ON PAGE 91

Hints and tips

- Intersperse shadowing sessions with activities that are more productive.
- Point out that the shadowing exercise is more to gain familiarity with the way your department works than a serious training exercise.
- A morning's or afternoon's shadowing is probably enough for one session.

Sit by Nellie

This is learning by simply watching someone who already knows the task and does it well ('Nellie'). This is one of the easiest methods for passing a skill on.

For	Against
■ good for introduction of simple repetitive tasks that do not need a lot of explanation	■ can be time-consuming for the developee; there is not much pressure to learn fast
■ *cheap* – there is no cost incurred and 'Nellie' keeps on working	■ the 'Nellie' might be so adept at the task that they do it too quickly for the observer to fully understand what is going on
■ the person being developed can learn at their own pace	■ there is sometimes a tendency to pass on 'short cuts' before the basic knowledge is achieved
■ the learning takes place in the 'real world' and so is likely to be better remembered	■ bad habits might be passed on as well as good habits.
■ it's good for 'Nellie' too; people love sharing their skills and one of the best ways to refine a skill is to have to demonstrate it to others.	

Finding help

'Nellies' need to be carefully chosen. Stay away from people who have a tendency to be impatient or abrupt – even though they may be absolute wizards at doing the task you need the developee to learn. It is better to choose someone with a rather more placid nature who will take the time to answer questions without becoming exasperated at being interrupted. Do not appoint a Nellie who is under time pressure and who has real deadlines to meet.

Setting it up

Brief the developee carefully on the following things:

- which task you want them to watch
- where this task fits into their job
- why this task is important and the impact it has on the rest of the job
- when the task will be handed over to them
- what latitude they have to alter the way that the task is done (in other words, how much they can alter the task to suit themselves)
- encourage them to ask questions.

Brief the Nellie on the following things:

- which task(s) you want them to demonstrate
- who they will be showing them to
- why it is important for the developee to know how to do this task(s)
- encouraging the developee to ask questions
- working to a rough timescale where possible
- when you are going to touch base with them to see how the developee is getting on.

Resources and people needed

- none really – 'Nellie-ing' is as cheap as it is effective.

Checking on learning

- Can the developee do the task? (Do not expect perfection too quickly!)
- Has the developee started to feel comfortable with the task?
- Has the developee found a way (if this is possible) to do the task more efficiently?

Similar activities

- apprenticeships used to be based on a great deal of sitting by Nellie
- shadowing, where a new employee accompanies a more experienced team member for a few days (see page 89).

Hints and tips

- If you are not sure about which tasks would be best learned through sitting by Nellie, ask the more experienced members of your team – they have probably been through the learning curve more recently than you.
- Do not ignore the need for development in apparently mundane tasks like telephone handling, passing messages on, filling in forms etc. These are probably second nature to you but might seem daunting to a school leaver or someone moving from a job that did not involve such activities.
- Always, always thank the Nellie personally – even though they have not really been inconvenienced by the 'Nellie-ing', they have still put effort into it – and you may want them to do it again in the future.

Supplier training

Take a look around the office. Photocopiers, printers, computers, filing systems, telephones, fax machines, stationery cupboards, office furniture, cameras, projectors – the list is a long one. Now think about the services you purchase: insurance, accountancy, tax advice, cleaning services – another long list. The companies that sell you these things are all experts in their own fields; they have knowledge and skills that would be useful to you and your team. Why not ask them to train your people? We once bought a really complicated photocopying machine for the office; it did everything except make the tea while it was colour copying, collating and binding. *Not one of us could make it work.* Oh, we had had a thorough demonstration but we still could not get the hang of it. In the end I rang the manufacturer and started to negotiate with them to swap the all-singing, all-dancing machine for a simpler version. I was amazed when the manufacturer offered us a free training course, to be delivered at our office to all of us. We took up the offer and it was excellent. After a day we were all completely comfortable with the machine.

This got us thinking. We had a new office junior who was learning to look after the office logistics. She was willing but very inexperienced and needed to learn about things like stock control, ordering and invoicing. 'Who would know about these things?' we thought. 'Our stationery supplier!' So we rang them, told them what we needed and they could not have been more helpful. The office junior went along to *their* offices for a couple of days and came back transformed! And it did not cost us a penny. Now while I am not suggesting that we should inundate our suppliers with demands for free training, it does seem to be a resource for development that could be used more often. Every salesperson has a silver lining.

For	Against
■ training by experts	■ they try to sell you things.
■ free or not expensive	
■ informal approach	
■ creates a strong bond with suppliers.	

Finding help

Be very clear what you want to achieve and then contact a really reliable supplier. Stress that you are not looking for formal training, mainly advice and expertise. I have found that the more successful the supplier, the more likely they are to offer help. Many salespeople are mines of information and can often be readily persuaded to run workshops for you if they know it will help them to make the sale.

Setting it up

- Define what you want.
- Work out what you can offer in return.
- Contact the supplier or their salesperson and see if they can help.

Resources and people needed

You may have to supply the logistics part of the training sessions and supply the space.

Similar activities

SEE *FIND THE EXPERT* ON PAGE 64

Hints and tips

- If you can offer a similar service to your suppliers they will be more inclined to help you when you need them.
- Do not expect polished training sessions – it is their expertise and experience you are after, not formal training courses.

Teach it back

This is where you really capitalise on the expertise within your team. One of the best ways of developing a skill is to have to teach it to someone else – particularly a new skill that you are trying to refine. The very activity of preparing a teaching session on a specific subject forces you to examine the processes you need to get through in order to achieve the right result. Training others improves your communication, problem-solving and selling skills. Since this is so like coaching (see page 42) and demonstration (see page 56) there is little more to be said, except that it really does make formal training cost-effective when an individual with newly acquired skills from a training course shares his or her new expertise with the rest of the group. This is also an excellent way for you as a manager to develop yourself. Try it and see!

Video feedback

There is nothing quite as useful as seeing yourself in action *from the outside*. Presentation skills courses regularly use video feedback to alert participants to correctable mistakes and habits. It is only after seeing yourself in full and colourful glory that you can really evaluate the multitude of things that are going on when you interact with others. The video camera is an excellent tool for self-development, particularly behavioural skills like interviewing, selling, chairing meetings, speaking to groups and training.

For	Against
■ gives people a chance to look at how they interact with others	■ it may take a while for people to get used to looking at themselves on a screen
■ shows progress being made	■ some people really hate looking at themselves on screen and can be demotivated by it.
■ can be used privately.	

Finding help

Choose the best-quality camera and playback equipment and lighting that you can find. A dull, flickering image is counterproductive. Make sure that help is at hand for people who are not familiar with the equipment (and for that reason, try to use cameras and playback kit that is easy to use).

Setting it up

- Set up the room so that the camera is far enough away from the person to be videoed to allow a full body image to be seen.
- Practise using the camera and work out just where to stand if you are videoing yourself on your own.
- Start recording (try not to perform only to the camera).
- Stop, rewind and have an immediate feedback session *before* you watch the tape.
- Play back.
- Analyse what you have seen and then repeat the 'performance', trying to correct your mistakes.

Resources and people needed

- a quiet, well-lit and uninterrupted space
- a video camera and tripod
- playback media (videotape and monitor or projector and screen)
- good lighting
- tapes.

Checking on learning

The evidence is on the tapes.

Similar activities

SEE *ROLE PLAY* ON PAGE 87

Hints and tips

- If you choose to have someone operating the camera for you, ask them to set the camera up and then stand away from it while it is recording, only going back to it if a close-up or zoom-out is needed. If the cameraperson stands by the camera it makes the camera too intrusive and less easy to forget. Believe it or not, after a few minutes people really do forget that they are being filmed.

■ Keep the camera running for the initial feedback session – these comments are often the most spontaneous ones.

■ Look at the tapes from time to time to remind yourself of your skills and weaknesses.

Videos/films

This last methodology is very like the first – audio tapes and CDs (see page 32). I can think of at least a dozen professional training companies that supply professional video films, most of them extremely effective. You can hire or buy these videos. There is no reason why you should not produce in-house videos yourself. The advantage of having a library of training videos is that your team can take them home whenever they need them so that they act as a way of both learning and reinforcing new skills. The reason I like professional videos is that the best video companies have amazing skills at their disposal – not just first-rate training designers, but performers who make the video a pleasure to use. I can still remember some of the punchlines from the very first management and sales videos I saw back in the 1980s (as indeed can my colleagues). Apart from passing on very valuable skills, they made us laugh so much that we never forgot them. A joke is often worth a million pages of theory.

Examples of groups of development options

I am loath to be prescriptive, since people's needs depend so much on the company, market and environment they work in – and not least their existing skills. It would be a mistake to think that manual workers only need manual skills, technical workers only need technical skills or knowledge workers only need intel-lectual skills. All of us have the potential to climb the manage-ment ladder and if we do we would need managerial experience and behavioural knowledge. All of us may well need to acquire a manual or technical skill as business tools are developed.

Having a working knowledge of how a machine works would help us to supervise others – even if we never actually worked at the machine itself.

The following examples are simply to show you how you could suggest a range of options that would broaden the complete skill range of an individual in certain circumstances.

Example 1

A new management trainee works in a large company specialising in the distribution of food. She is moving from working as a supervisor in the warehouse to running a team of five supervisors.

Find a **mentor** for her. Start her individual development with **shadowing** or **learning by walking about**, concentrating on visiting similar management teams. When she is comfortable with what her management duties entail, get her to form a **best practice group**. Start **delegating** simple managerial tasks to her. Get her to **sit by Nellie** on job interviews. **Find the expert** who knows about time management and logistics . . .

Example 2

A school leaver has just joined the engineering division of a company specialising in manufacturing small machine parts. He will eventually be part of a team producing four different machine parts.

Put him through a simple **induction** process. Get him to **sit by Nellie** on the production line for a couple of days. Get the other team members to **demonstrate** how to use the machines. Have the most accomplished machine worker **coach** him on actually how to use the machines. Make sure all **manuals and reference books** are available for him (if that is the way he is happy learning) . . .

Example 3

A new saleswoman has just joined your group. She has considerable selling experience, but knows nothing of your company or its products. She will be working in a market that is very familiar to her, but that your team knows nothing about.

Put her through a comprehensive **induction** process. Find an **audio tape** for her that she can play in her car that will bring her up to speed on product knowledge. Send her off to **learn by walking about** in the product development department. Get her to run a **coaching** session with the rest of the team where she can share her knowledge of the new market with the rest of you. Find her a **mentor** . . .

WHERE NEXT?

Here is a wish list, taken from the best managers I know. I asked them:

'What factors would make your life easier in terms of equipping your people to handle the changes that happen in your business all the time?'

This is what they said:

- ■ 'More time to spend on people issues.'
- ■ 'To be targeted and measured on managing people issues and not only on turnover and making the budget.'
- ■ 'More advance notice of company changes – more time to be involved in the big decisions that personally affect my people.'
- ■ 'More space – meeting rooms and quiet spaces.'
- ■ 'To be given realistic budgets and timescales, so that time for development can be scheduled in, rather than taking last place as an "extra" activity only when you can squeeze it in.'
- ■ 'Help with assessment interviews, development plans and recruitment.'
- ■ 'A bigger training budget – actually, a bigger *everything* budget.'
- ■ 'Superpeople – who can do everything that you throw at them – plus 36 hours in every day.' (This was said with a *very* wry smile.)

Again and again the response was to do with time – time to think, time to plan development activities, time to be involved in personal coaching, time to discuss with other managers the real 'people' needs of the business.

It was not that these managers were in any way unaware of the necessary profit element of business; it was that very often the imperatives of profit militated against the attempts to consider and fulfil the needs of the people in their companies.

To put it another way, this is what the CEO I quoted at the beginning of the book said:

There are three elements in business:

THE MARKET
THE PRODUCT
THE PEOPLE WHO MAKE OR SUPPLY THE PRODUCT

Without a market, you don't have a business. Without a product you don't have a business. And it's not much use having a market and product to suit if you can't produce it. BUT, you can have a really poor market for a while, or a poor product for a while but both can be compensated for by the right people ...I believe that you can sometimes get by even if you get things wildly wrong, provided you have the right people who will work to get them right.

Our task as a manager is to create the environment in which each individual can reach their potential.

From the options given in Section 3, you will see that with a little concentrated effort you will be able to set in train activities and exercises that do not necessarily involve large amounts of your time, but have tremendous payback in terms of increasing your team's knowledge and skills. From that increasing skill and knowledge base, there will follow a direct contribution to your company's bottom line. Indeed you will create the environment in which each individual can and will reach their full potential.

And so, on to the final question:

- 'How do we develop ourselves?'

The answer? Well, there is a lovely character in Charles Kingsley's *The Water Babies* by the name of Mrs Doasyouwouldbedoneby. So try some of the development options for yourself. All of them are useful at any level and all of them will broaden and deepen your own skills and knowledge base. Do not leave yourself out of the loop – all of your team will be behind you – sometimes snapping at your heels!

Try **learning by walking about**, have a go at **job swapping**, run a **case studies** session, become a **mentor**, have a look at what is available on the **Internet**. There is not a single option mentioned in Section 3 that would not be useful to you, and many that by the simple act of setting them up and monitoring them will develop you personally.

Henry Kissinger said:

> *A leader has to take people from where they are to where they have never been before.*

And *that* is what developing yourself and your people is all about.

INDEX

With over 100,000 members, the **Chartered Institute of Personnel and Development** is the largest organisation in Europe dealing with the management and development of people. The CIPD operates its own publishing unit, producing books and research reports for human resource practitioners, students, and general managers charged with people management responsibilities.

Currently there are over 150 titles, covering the full range of personnel and development issues. The books have been commissioned from leading experts in the field and are packed with the latest information and guidance to best practice.

For free copies of the CIPD Books Catalogue, please contact the publishing department:
Tel: 020 8263 3387
Fax: 020 8263 3850
E-mail: *publish@cipd.co.uk*
Web: *www.cipd.co.uk*

Orders for books should be sent direct to:
Plymbridge Distributors
Estover
Plymouth
Devon PL6 7PY
Tel: +44 (0) 1752 202301
Fax: +44 (0) 1752 202333
E-mail: orders@plymbridge.com

20 Ways to Manage Better
by
Andrew Leigh
(Third Edition)

This publication provides expert guidance on a series of crucial management issues. It focuses on the day-to-day aspects of a manager's role and provides endless hints and tips for action. This dependable title continues to avoid faddism and 'hot' topics, concentrating instead on providing guidance on core management issues.

This edition has been revised and updated so that now:

■ each chapter concludes with a list of recommended websites relevant to the chapter content – sites that help the reader pursue their interest in the topic concerned
■ important new guidance is given on issues around the Internet, talent management and changing styles of leadership
■ there is an extended reading list for further reading
■ more case examples are included.

March 2001   368 pages   ISBN 0 85292 879 3   **£13.99**

Improve Your People Skills
by
Peter Honey

In this celebrated mini-encyclopaedia, Peter Honey provides clear, concrete advice on how to:

■ be assertive, empower others and satisfy customers
■ release creativity, generate ideas – and build on them to solve problems
■ prevent anger, boredom, guilt and other unwanted feelings
■ praise, criticise and negotiate more effectively
■ cope with conflict.

Improve Your People Skills now includes a powerful diagnostic quiz to focus thinking on the best places to start.

March 2001   240 pages   ISBN 0 85292 903 X   **£12.99**

Everyone Needs a Mentor
by
David Clutterbuck
(Third Edition)

Everyone Needs a Mentor will help every employer to realise the potential of their best employees through the proven discipline of mentoring. This third edition has been fully revised and updated. David Clutterbuck provides detailed and practical advice on every stage of the process, from matching mentors and mentees through to identifying when the mentoring relationship should come to an end. He addresses fundamental questions, including:

- Who benefits from mentoring?
- How formal should the mentoring scheme be?
- How are mentoring schemes developed and managed?
- What are the key phases of the mentoring relationship?
- What problems may be encountered in mentoring programmes and relationships?

August 2001   ISBN 0 85292 904 8   **£12.99**